Culture

Raymond Williams was born in 1921 at the Welsh border village of Pandy. Educated at Abergavenny Grammar School and at Trinity College, Cambridge, he served in the war as an anti-tank captain in the Guards Armoured Division. After the war he was appointed an adult education tutor in the Oxford University delegacy for extra-mural studies. In 1961 he was elected fellow of Jesus College, Cambridge, and university lecturer in English. From 1974 until 1983 he was Professor of Drama at Cambridge, where he taught until his death in 1990.

His Published books include *Drama in Performance* (1954), *Culture and Society 1780-1950* (1958), *Border Country*, a novel (1960), *The Long Revolution* (1961), *Modern Tragedy* (1966), *Drama from Ibsen to Brecht* (1968), *The Country and the City* (1973), *Marxism and Literature* (1977), *The Volunteers*, a novel (1978), *Towards 2000* (1983), *Writing in Society* (1983), *Resource of Hope* (1989) and *What I Came to Say* (1989).

Also available from Fontana Press are his *Keywords* and his Modern Master on *Orwell*.

Raymond Williams

Culture

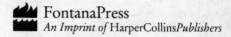

FontanaPress
An Imprint of HarperCollins*Publishers*

Fontana Press
An Imprint of HarperCollins*Publishers*
77–85 Fulham Palace Road,
Hammersmith, London W6 8JB

Published by Fontana Press 1981
9 8 7 6 5

ISBN 0 00 686099 0

Set in Plantin

Printed in Great Britain by
HarperCollinsManufacturing, Glasgow

Contents

Editor's Preface

This series is designed to provide comprehensive and authoritative analyses of issues at the centre of contemporary sociological discussion. Each volume will therefore present and evaluate both the major theoretical standpoints and the empirical findings relevant to specific problems within sociology: but, in addition, each volume will itself be an original contribution to our understanding of that topic. So the series will be of value to laymen and professional sociologists alike.

The focus will be on contemporary Britain, although comparison with the institutional orders of other advanced societies and, indeed, with pre-capitalist social formations, will form an integral part of each book. Analyses of the division of labour, its structure and consequences, of social class and other forms of inequality, and of the institutions and the distribution of power in politics and in industry, will dominate the collection. Yet this emphasis will not preclude discussion of other aspects of contemporary British society, such as the family, urbanism or law-breaking.

The series is based on three premises. First the primary concern of sociology as an academic discipline is the analysis of *social structure* – of the institutions and social processes characteristic of advanced industrial societies. Second, the distinction between 'sociological theory' and 'empirical sociology', found so often within the subject, is false. Finally, sociological explanation incorporates historical explanation; and 'social' institutions cannot be examined in isolation from 'economic' or 'political' ones. Indeed, one of the most important changes now taking place in the social sciences is the recognition that the boundaries which hitherto have separated one discipline from another are artificial. On these premises, the series determines to help us understand the functioning of the society in which we live.

Gavin Mackenzie
Jesus College, Cambridge

1 Towards a Sociology of Culture

The sociology of culture, in its most recent and most active forms, has to be seen as a convergence of very different interests and methods. Like other convergences, it includes at least as many collisions and near misses as genuine meeting points. But so many people, in many countries, are now working in it that it has entered a new phase.

Within traditional categories the sociology of culture is seen as a doubtful area. In ordinary lists of the fields of sociology it gets in, if at all, as a very late entry: not only after the hard stuff of class, industry and politics, of the family or of crime, but as a miscellaneous heading after the more defined fields of the sociology of religion, education and knowledge.

It then both seems and is underdeveloped. There is no actual shortage of specific studies, though here, as elsewhere, much more remains to be done. It is rather that until it is recognized as a convergence, and as a problem of convergence, the usual reaction, even when sympathetic (and this, among an older and established generation, is comparatively rare) is to see it as little more than a loose grouping of specialist studies either of communications, in their modern specialized form as 'the media', or of the rather differently specialized field of 'the arts'.

Of course to see these studies as specialist, in a working

and practical sense, is quite reasonable. But to see them as marginal or peripheral is something else again. The modern convergence, which the contemporary sociology of culture embodies, is in fact an attempt to rework, from a particular set of interests, those general social and sociological ideas within which it has been possible to see communication, language and art as marginal and peripheral, or as at best secondary and derived social processes. A modern sociology of culture, whether in its internal studies or in its interventions in a more general sociology, is concerned above all to enquire, actively and openly, into these received and presumed relations, and into other possible and demonstrable relations. As such it is not only reworking its own field, but putting new questions and new evidence into the general work of the social sciences.

'Culture'

Both the problem and the interest of the sociology of culture can be seen at once in the difficulty of its apparently defining term: 'culture'. The history and usage of this exceptionally complex term can be studied in Kroeber and Kluckhohn (1952) and Williams (1958 and 1976). Beginning as a noun of *process* – the culture (cultivation) of crops or (rearing and breeding) of animals, and by extension the culture (active cultivation) of the human mind – it became in the late eighteenth century, especially in German and English, a noun of *configuration* or *generalization* of the 'spirit' which informed the 'whole way of life' of a distinct people. Herder (1784–91) first used the significant plural, 'cultures', in deliberate distinction from any singular or, as we would now say, unilinear sense of 'civilization'. The broad pluralist term was then especially important in the nineteenth-century development of comparative anthropology, where it has continued to designate a whole and distinctive way of life.

But there are then fundamental questions about the nature of the formative or determining elements which produce these distinctive cultures. Alternative answers to these questions have produced a range of effective meanings, both within anthropology and in extension from it: from the older emphasis on an 'informing spirit' – ideal or religious or national – to more modern emphases on a 'lived culture' which has been primarily determined by other and now differently designated social processes – usually particular kinds of political or economic order. In the alternative and contending intellectual traditions which have flowed from this range of answers, 'culture' itself then ranges from a significantly total to a confidently partial dimension of reference.

Meanwhile, in more general usage, there was a strong development of the sense of 'culture' as the active cultivation of the mind. We can distinguish a range of meanings from (i) *a developed state of mind* – as in 'a person of culture', 'a cultured person' to (ii) *the processes of this development* – as in 'cultural interests', 'cultural activities' to (iii) *the means of these processes* – as in culture as 'the arts' and 'humane intellectual works'. In our own time (iii) is the most common general meaning, though all are current. It coexists, often uneasily, with the anthropological and extended sociological use to indicate the 'whole way of life' of a distinct people or other social group.

The difficulty of the term is then obvious, but can be most usefully seen as the result of earlier kinds of convergence of interests. We can distinguish two main kinds: (a) an emphasis on the *'informing spirit'* of a whole way of life, which is manifest over the whole range of social activities but is most evident in 'specifically cultural' activities – a language, styles of art, kinds of intellec tual work; and (b) an emphasis on 'a whole social order' within which a specifiable culture, in styles of art and kinds of intellectual work, is seen as the direct or indirect product of an order primarily constituted by other social activities.

These positions are often classified as (a) *idealist* and (b) *materialist*, though it should be noted that in (b) materialist explanation is commonly reserved to the other, 'primary', activities, leaving 'culture' to a version of the 'informing spirit', of course now differently based and not primary but secondary. Yet the importance of each position, by contrast with other forms of thought, is that it leads, necessarily, to intensive study of the relations between 'cultural' activities and other forms of social life. Each position implies a broad method: in (a) illustration and clarification of the 'informing spirit', as in national histories of styles of art and kinds of intellectual work which manifest, in relation with other institutions and activities, the central interests and values of a 'people'; in (b) exploration from the known or discoverable character of a general social order to the specific forms taken by its cultural manifestations.

The sociology of culture, as it entered the second half of the twentieth century, was broadly compounded of work done from these two positions, much of it of great local value. Each position represented a form of that convergence of interests which the term 'culture' itself, with its persistent range of relational emphases, notably exemplifies. But in contemporary work, while each of the earlier positions is still held and practised, a new kind of convergence is becoming evident.

This has many elements in common with (b), in its emphasis on a whole social order, but it differs from it in its insistence that 'cultural practice' and 'cultural production' (its most recognizable terms) are not simply derived from an otherwise constituted social order but are themselves major elements in its constitution. It then shares some elements with (a), in its emphasis on cultural practices as (though now among others) *constitutive*. But instead of the 'informing spirit' which was held to constitute all other activities, it sees culture as the *signifying system* through which necessarily (though among óther means) a social order is communicated, reproduced, experienced and explored.

Thus there is some practical convergence between (i) the anthropological and sociological senses of culture as a distinct 'whole way of life', within which, now, a distinctive 'signifying system' is seen not only as essential but as essentially involved in *all* forms of social activity, and (ii) the more specialized if also more common sense of culture as 'artistic and intellectual activities', though these, because of the emphasis on a general signifying system, are now much more broadly defined, to include not only the traditional arts and forms of intellectual production but also all the 'signifying practices' – from language through the arts and philosophy to journalism, fashion and advertising – which now constitute this complex and necessarily extended field.

This book is written within the terms of this contemporary convergence. In some of its chapters, notably 4, 5, 7 and 8, it deals with questions over its whole range. In its other chapters, while conscious of the general field, it deliberately concentrates on 'the arts' in their most common received sense. The work of the new convergence has been best and most frequently done, either in general theory and in studies of 'ideology', or in its distinctively new areas of interest, in 'the media' and 'popular culture'. There is then not only a relative gap to be filled, in these new terms, but also, from the quality of some of the work on the arts carried out from other positions, a sense of challenge: indeed a sense that it may be above all in this still major area that the qualities of the kinds of thinking represented by the contemporary convergence stand most to be tested.

Why a 'sociology' of culture?

It will already be clear that in the contemporary convergence, with its deliberate extension and interlocking of hitherto separate (if always related) senses of culture, what is now often called 'cultural studies' is already a branch of general sociology. But it is a branch more in the sense of a distinctive mode of entry into general sociological questions than in the sense of a reserved or specialized area. At the same time, while it is a kind of sociology which places its emphasis on all signifying systems, it is necessarily and centrally concerned with manifest cultural practices and production. Its whole approach requires, as we shall see, new kinds of social analysis of specifically cultural institutions and formations, and the exploration of actual relations between these and, on the one hand, the material means of cultural production and, on the other hand, actual cultural forms. What brings these together is, distinctively, a sociology, but, in the terms of the convergence, a sociology of a new kind.

We have already seen the theoretical differences between this and earlier forms of convergence. We can now indicate, if only in outline, the historical forms of the same development. The new sociology of culture can be seen as the convergence, and at a certain point the transformation, of two clear tendencies: one within general social thought and then specifically sociology; the other within cultural history and analysis. We can briefly indicate the major contributions within each.

The 'cultural sciences' and sociology

It was Vico, in his *New Science* (1725–44), who gave at once a new confidence and a particular direction to social thought, in his argument that 'the world of civil society has certainly been made by men' and that this 'since men had made it they could hope to know'. What thus far was a general argument for the validity of all social sciences was given a special emphasis by Vico's idea of finding the 'principles' of civil society 'within the modifications of our own human mind'. For if the human mind is *modified*, in and through social development, it is a necessary emphasis of social studies to examine the cultural forms – for Vico, notably, language – through which social development is manifested.

This is so again in Herder (1784–91), who added the concept of specific cultural forms, but in a context, already discussed, of the 'informing. spirit'. There are clear continuities from both Vico and Herder in Dilthey (1883), who offered an important distinction between 'the cultural sciences' (*Geisteswissenschaften*) and 'the natural sciences'. He distinguished the cultural sciences by the fact that their 'objects of study' are humanly made, that someone observing them is observing processes in which he himself necessarily participates, and that different methods of establishing evidence and interpretations are then inevitable. Specifically Dilthey defined method through the difficult concept of '*verstehen*' – a 'sympathetic understanding' or 'intuitive grasp' of human social and cultural forms – while at the same time insisting that all such studies must be historical. This emphasis passed into the work of Max Weber and thus into one tendency in modern sociology.

But quite different ideas were also contributing to the

formation of modern sociology. These stressed the discovery, by the different method of objective observation and recording (often by analogy with the natural sciences), of the laws of social organization. There were strengths and weaknesses in each of these tendencies. The method of '*verstehen*' could be quite insufficiently explanatory, or could fall back for explanation on a (theoretically circular) 'informing spirit'. The method of objective observation, while accumulating indispensable empirical data, was often insufficiently conscious of the nature of some of the less tangible cultural processes, of these as elements of history and, crucially, of the effects on observation of the specific social and cultural situation of the observer.

These problems, in more refined forms, have continued to exercise sociological theory, but their effects on the sociology of culture are now most relevant. The study of cultural forms and works continued, by an obvious affinity, to be practised by exponents of '*verstehen*'. Elsewhere, within mainstream sociology, the cultural facts which were most amenable to observational analysis were primarily institutions and the cultural 'products' of institutions. Within sociology generally, these were the persistent emphases of the two earlier historical convergences. Each contributed much, but they did not often speak to each other, and indeed almost literally could not speak to each other.

1 Contributions from observational sociology

Thus we find in the tradition of observational analysis (which in Britain and America is often taken as sociology *tout court*) a developing interest in cultural institutions at that point when, through actual social developments in the modern press, cinema and broadcasting, there were major institutions and their products which could be studied by already generally available methods. In this tradition, before this development, the sociology of culture had significantly been concentrated on the already institutionalized areas of religion and education. Three useful kinds of study can then be distinguished, of (i) the social and economic institutions of culture and, as alternative definitions of their 'products', of (ii) their content and (iii) their effects.

(i) Institutions

There have been many studies of modern communications institutions within one explicitly (functional) sociological perspective. For examples see Lasswell (1948), Lazarsfeld and Merton (1948), Lazarsfeld and Stanton (1949). Other studies of the same institutions combine institutional analysis with some history – White (1947) – or with general social argument – Siebert, Peterson and Schramm (1956). It is significant that in this area of institutional studies some of the sharpest questions about the nature of sociological inquiry have been directly or indirectly posed. Much of the earlier American work, highly developed empirically and in its immediate working concepts, was undertaken within a relatively uncritical assumption of a market society, where general 'socializing' and 'commercial' functions could be supposed to interact or conflict. It was also commonly described by an interpretation of modern society as 'mass society', in which such different elements as very large audiences, relative 'impersonality' of transmission or 'anonymity' of reception, and the 'unorganized heterogeneity' of 'democratic and commercial' societies were fused and indeed confused. This assumption led to the designation and methodology of 'mass communication' research, which still dominates the orthodox sociology of culture. For a critique of the concept and its effects, see Williams (1974).

Ironically, the same concept and designation were evident in work of a different kind, where comparable observational and analytic techniques were employed but in the context of a radical critique of the institutions and their functions in *capitalist* society (a specification of particular kinds of 'socialization' and 'communication' within a particular social and economic order). This explicitly campaigning sociology was of course in conflict with the (only apparently) 'neutral' stance of the earlier phase. It added, necessarily, elements of economic analysis (of the ownership of institutions) and of economic and political history. A major example is Schiller (1969), but see also Weinberg (1962), Murdock and Golding (1974) and Glasgow University Media Group (1976).

There have been relatively few studies of modern cultural institutions outside the dominant fields of press and broadcasting, but on cinema see Mayer (1948) and on more recent approaches see Albrecht, Barnett and Griff (1970). Empirical studies of older cultural institutions, drawing on historical as well as sociological procedures, include Collins (1928), Beljame (1948), Altick (1957), Williams (1961) and Escarpit (1966).

(ii) Content

Sociological studies of cultural 'content' have been distinguished from otherwise comparable studies, in the history of art or of literature, by the methodological assumptions of observational analysis. Thus 'content analysis' has been defined as 'a research technique for the objective, systematic and quantitative description of the manifest content of communications' (Wright [1959], 76). This work has been useful in two main areas: analysis of types of content – see Berelson (1950) and Williams (1962) – and of the selection and portrayal of certain social figures

– see Lowenthal (1961). In the former case, analysis
necessarily requires extensive and systematic survey
procedures, by contrast with the more selective and even
arbitrary treatment of 'content' in non-sociological studies
This is true also of the latter case, where the cultural
research into fictional 'types' can be combined with
broader analysis of the changing social significance of
certain socially 'typical' figures (policeman and detective,
doctor, nurse, priest, criminal and so on).

Content analysis is often criticized for its 'merely
quantitative' findings, but its data, while often needing
further interpretation, are essential to any developed
sociology of culture, not only in modern communications
systems, where the large numbers of works make it
inevitable, but also in more traditional kinds of work.

(iii) Effects

The most evident contributions of observational sociology
have been in the study of effects. This tendency is itself in
need of sociological analysis, since it is in some respects
clearly related to the social character of certain modern
institutions, most obviously in advertising and market
research but also in audience research and in political
opinion polling. Funding for research of this kind has been
on a scale not approached by any other area of sociological
enquiry. But we can then distinguish between two kinds of
study: (a) *operational studies*, often not generally published,
which study effects as indicators of internal policy and
marketing decisions – 'attitude' surveys in market research; studies of responses to programmes in broadcasting research; private political polling on 'issues'; and (b)
critical research, in which the effects of programmes
showing violence or of political broadcasting or other
distinguishable kinds of production are assessed for both
specific and general social effect, often in response to an

expressed public concern. Much of what we now know, in a still difficult and very controversial area, about different kinds of 'televised violence' and their differential effects on differently situated children, or about the effects of different kinds of political broadcasting – party statements, electoral reporting, definitions of the 'main issues' – has come from this kind of research. For examples see Himmelweit, Oppenheim and Vince (1958), Blumler and McQuail (1968), and, more generally, Lazarsfeld and Katz (1955), Halloran (1970) and Halloran, Brown and Chaney (1970).

A critique of 'effects studies', raising the question of the social norms on which the effects are presumed to operate, is in Williams (1974). At the same time it should be remembered that in non-sociological cultural studies, as in much general writing, the question of effect is commonly raised but without much or any evidence and often by simple and even casual assertion. Here, as elsewhere, the sociological contribution, while usually needing critique and refinement, has been indispensable.

2 The alternative tradition

Outside observational sociology there was an early convergence between social theories of culture and what had been more specifically philosophical, historical and critical theories and studies of art. This was especially so in the German tradition, where several important schools developed. And it was from the beginning the case in a more general Marxist tradition, which has been especially active and, it should be stressed, diverse in recent years.

Before turning to this complex modern area, we should note certain major examples of cultural history and analysis which we would not call sociological but in which some crucial concepts and methods were practically explored. Outstanding among these, in addition to the work of Vico and Herder already discussed, are Ruskin (1851–6 and 1857) and Burckhardt (translated 1878), together with the work of Dilthey (translated 1976). It can be said that works of this kind – and there are many other possible examples – begin more evidently from the actual art and culture in question, and can thus be assigned to history or criticism. Yet they are distinct from general art history and criticism in their conscious introduction, if in varying ways, of active social concepts as necessary elements of description and analysis. Their overlap with modern cultural sociology, in the alternative tradition, is thus clear.

In modern studies we can distinguish three broad emphases: (i) on the social conditions of art; (ii) on social material in art works; and (iii) on social relations in art works.

(i) Social conditions of art

Work on the social conditions of art overlaps, evidently, with general aesthetics and some branches of psychology, as well as with history. Indeed there is a major theoretical division, within such work, between primarily aesthetic and psychological approaches, on the one hand, and primarily historical approaches on the other. Some work of the former kind altogether avoids social considerations, and passes out of our present context. But there are significant tendencies based primarily on 'aesthetic' and 'psychological' data which either (a) introduce social conditions as modifiers of an otherwise relatively constant human process or (b) construct general periods of human culture within which certain types of art flourish. Examples of the former include Read (1936) and other works of a generally 'social-Freudian' orientation; of the latter, with some precedents in Nietzsche (1872) and Frazer

(1890), in Weston (1920), Jung (1933) and Frye (1957).

The most interesting current aspect of work of this kind, which in general bears decisively away from sociology and indeed is often hostile to it, is its relation to one tendency in Marxist thinking about art. Neither Marx nor Engels wrote systematically about art, but important theoretical positions were derived from them. The best known of these positions relate to analyses of social material and social relations in art works, and will be discussed below. But there is Marxist work on the origins and on typologies of art which properly belongs in this first division. Examples include Plekhanov (translated 1953), relating art to 'primitive instincts' or 'drives', Kautsky (1927), relating the development of art to evolved animal behaviour, Caudwell (1938), relating art to the 'genotype', and Fischer (1963). Elements of these approaches, combined (as also in Caudwell) with specifically historical orientations, can be seen in Lukács (1969) and Marcuse (1978).

It is important to distinguish work of this kind, and to emphasize its possible value, by comparison with that narrowest version of the social conditions of art (often called 'sociologism' or 'sociological relativism'), which is more commonly associated with Marxism. No studies of art can in the end neglect the physical processes and needs of the human organism, with which (see Chapter 4) its means of production are so closely involved. These can be directly studied in physiology and experimental psychology, but there is then the major problem of the variability of the kinds of work produced from these (presumably) common bases, in the evidence of anthropology and of history. Correlations in this area, especially in non-Marxist work but still in most Marxist work hitherto, have tended to proceed less from the steady analysis of evidence than from relatively *a priori* concepts, usually of a strictly contemporary kind, to which such evidence as there is is illustratively added. This is especially the case in the abstraction of 'magical practices' or of 'economic motives' or 'sexual symbolism' to give generic explanations of the art of other cultures. All these concepts have been applied, successively, to prehistoric cave paintings, with different but always arbitrary results. Meanwhile the abstraction of an 'aesthetic instinct', isolated from its conditions and from other relationships, has, while often coming nearer to the work, suppressed the whole problem of connected but variable practices.

Substantial theoretical correctives to such procedures can be found in the important work of Mukarovsky (translated 1970) and Morawski (1974). In terms of the sociology of culture, this area can now be theoretically redefined as a study of the situations and conditions of practices (see Chapter 4). We have then to look in detail at the ways in which relatively constant biological processes and relatively variable means of production have combined both in specifically comparable and in specifically variable ways, always within specific social (historico-social) situations. Yet by comparison with the bodies of conceptual speculation, this fundamental sociology of culture has barely begun.

(ii) Social material in art works

The study of social material in art works has been very extensive, and is often taken, simply, as the whole content of a sociology of culture. Much of it, in fact, is more properly historical, but it includes one major sociological formulation or assumption. This is most recognizable in the theory of 'base and superstructure', effectively generalized for culture by Plekhanov (translated 1953). The problems of this concept are discussed in Williams (1977). Within this tendency, the basic 'facts' or 'structure' of a given society and/or period are received or are established by general analysis, and their 'reflection' in actual works is more or less directly traced. Thus both the content and the form of the new eighteenth-century realist novel can be shown as dependent on the already known facts of the increasing social importance of the commercial bourgeoisie. For a sustained and influential example of this method, see Lukács (1950).

(iii) Social relations in art works

At its most complex, the analysis of social material in art extends into the study of social relations. This is especially so when the idea of 'reflection' – in which art works directly embody pre-existing social material – is modified or replaced by the idea of 'mediation'.

Mediation can refer primarily to the necessary processes of composition, in a specific medium; as such it indicates the practical relations between social and artistic forms (see below). But in its more common uses it refers to an indirectness of relation between experience and its composition. The form of this indirectness is variably interpreted in different uses of the concept. Thus Kafka's novel *The Trial*, for example, can be read, from different positions, as (a) *mediation by projection* – an arbitrary and irrational social system is not directly described, in its own terms, but projected, in its essentials, as strange and alien; or (b) *mediation by the discovery of an 'objective correlative'* – a situation and characters are composed to produce, in an objective form, the subjective or actual feelings – an inexpressible guilt – from which the original impulse to composition came; or (c) *mediation as a function of the fundamental social processes of consciousness*, in which certain crises which cannot otherwise be directly apprehended are 'crystallized' in certain direct images and forms of art – images which then illuminate a basic (social and psychological) condition: not just Kafka's but a general alienation. In (c) this 'basic condition' can be variably referred to the nature of a whole epoch, of a particular society at a particular period, or of a particular group within that society at that period. All these references, but most obviously the second and especially the third, are potentially sociological, but they involve very different kinds of analysis from the tracing of direct relations of content or of form. Analyses employing these concepts and methods can be found in Benjamin (translated 1969), Goldmann (1964), Adorno (1967a) and the collective work of the important Frankfurt School (see Jay, 1973).

Forms

There has been some convergence between the analysis of social material and social relations in art works and the content-analysis of communications material described above. In their assumption of systematically traceable content, either reflected or mediated, they have considerable common ground, and between them have produced much valuable work. But there has in recent years been a more influential convergence, both in studies of art and in communications studies, around the concept of 'forms'. This emphasis has been notably theorized and exemplified in Lukács (translated 1971), Goldmann (translated 1975) and in Bloch *et al.* (translated 1977) where it is also vigorously debated. An extended discussion of this kind of social analysis is in Chapters 5 and 6.

Forms and social relations

From the analysis of what can be defined, within this tendency, as the social forms of art, there has been some development of the analysis of their corresponding social formations. There is a good example in Goldmann (1964), and there are classic pioneering studies in Gramsci (translated 1971) and Benjamin (translated 1973). Here again there is some convergence with the work of a more directly sociological tradition, and especially (though many theoretical problems are then raised) with Mannheim (1936 and 1956), as well as with a number of empirical studies of specific groups and conditions (cf. Beljame [1948]). The sociology of *cultural formations*, and its relations with the more widely practised sociology of *institutions*, is directly investigated in Chapters 2 and 3.

Ideology

It remains to indicate one especially important and difficult area of the sociology of culture, which has been prominent and at times dominant in the current convergence. This is the set of problems associated with the difficult term 'ideology'.

'Ideology' is an indispensable term in sociological analysis, but the first level of difficulty is whether it is used to describe: (a) the *formal and conscious beliefs* of a class or other social group – as in the common usage of 'ideological' to indicate general principles or theoretical positions or, as so often unfavourably, dogmas; or (b) the characteristic *world-view or general perspective* of a class or other social group, which will include formal and conscious beliefs but also less conscious, less formulated attitudes, habits and feelings, or even unconscious assumptions, bearings and commitments.

It is clear, first, that sociological analysis of culture has often, even primarily, to work with sense (a). It is a main way in which cultural production can be related, often very precisely, to social classes and other groups which can also be defined in other social terms, by political or economic or occupational analysis. But it is soon clear, also, that cultural analysis cannot be confined to the level of formal and conscious beliefs.

Two kinds of extension are necessary. First, to that wider area of feelings and attitudes and assumptions which usually mark, very distinctively, the culture of a particular class or other group. This wider and less tangible area is also important in tracing the changing culture of what is otherwise (say in economic terms) a continuing or persistent class. In such areas we discover a whole lived 'colouring', and a wide area of actual social practice, which are culturally specific and thus analytically indispensable. Then, second, there is need for extension to that area of manifest cultural production which, by the nature of its forms, is not, or not primarily or only, the expression of formal and conscious beliefs: not philosophy or religion or economic theory or political theory or law, but drama, fiction, poetry, painting.

There are often in fact close connections between the formal and conscious beliefs of a class or other group and the cultural production associated with it: sometimes direct connections with the beliefs, in included manifest content; often traceable connections to the relations, perspectives and values which the beliefs legitimize or normalize, as in characteristic selections (emphases and omissions) of subject; often, again, analysable connections between belief-systems and artistic forms, or between both and an essentially underlying 'position and positioning' in the world.

But then the use of 'ideology' as a common term in these essentially different stages of analysis can be confused and confusing. In the case of manifest content there is no real problem. Characteristic selectivities can also, without much strain, be called 'ideological', though something must often be allowed for an otherwise conditioned persistence of certain artistic forms embodying such selections. It is in the case of deeper congruences and possible congruences that the use of 'ideology' raises most problems, since if ideology is a major reference-point, or even point of origin, at such basic levels of social production and reproduction, it is difficult, as previously in some uses of 'culture', to know what is left for all other social processes.

Moreover, while 'ideology' retains, from the weight of linguistic usage, the sense of organized beliefs (whether formal and conscious or pervasive and dissolved), it can often be supposed that such systems are the true origin of all cultural (and indeed other social) production. In the case of art this would be very seriously reductive. It would exclude, on the one hand, the directly physical and material processes (cf. Chapter 4) in which so many arts are grounded. It would exclude, on the other hand, those crucial processes of working and reworking which are the specifics, as distinct from the *abstractable* elements, of important art. These processes range from (a) active illustration (still relatively simple) to (b) kinds of active reinvention and exploratory discovery and, crucially, (c) tension, contradiction or what would elsewhere be called dissent. They range also from what can be seen, simply, as the 'translation' of 'ideology' into directly sensuous material, to what is better seen, in terms of the physical and material processes of art work, as *production* of a distinct and general kind.

We have then to note that, unless we make these extensions and qualifications, 'ideology', even and perhaps especially in some powerful contemporary tendencies in Marxist analysis, is in effect repeating the history of 'culture' as a concept. In its more specific uses it has much to contribute by way of correction to generalizing uses of 'culture'. It can break down what is often the false generality of a 'whole way of life' to discriminate ascriptions to specific classes and other groups. As such indeed it is a key procedural term in an active sociology of culture. But in its more extended and generalized uses it can become remarkably similar to the 'informing spirit' of idealist cultural theories, and this can still be so when it offers (but does not include or specify) a 'last instance' referral to the economy or to the mode of production.

It is not the generality as such that is at fault. General ideologies, in their full depth and elaboration, have indeed to be seen as among the most remarkable forms of collective cultural production. But then it is precisely because all significant ideologies are indeed this deep and elaborated that the concept cannot be abstracted as some kind of 'informing spirit', at the roots of all cultural production. To say that all cultural practice is 'ideological' need mean no more than that (as in some other current uses) all practice is signifying. For all the difficulties of overlap with other more common uses, this sense is acceptable. But it is very different from describing all cultural production as 'ideology', or as 'directed by ideology', because what is then omitted, as in the idealist uses of 'culture', is the set of complex real processes by which a 'culture' or an 'ideology' is itself produced. And it is with these productive processes that a full sociology of culture is necessarily concerned. To study 'an ideology' and what 'it' produces is a recognizable form of idealist philosophy. What the cultural sociologist or the cultural historian studies are the social practices and social relations which produce not only 'a culture' or 'an ideology' but, more significantly, those dynamic actual states and works within which there are not only continuities and persistent determinations but also tensions, conflicts, resolutions and irresolutions, innovations and actual changes.

One final point can be made about current uses of 'ideology'. Where it is contrasted, as 'false consciousness' or as 'illusory experience' with 'science' (cf. Althusser [1970, 1971]) it is often remarkably similar, in effect, to that presumed area of 'common experience' against which the 'scientific observation' of empirical sociology positioned itself. To be sure, the philosophical bases of these tendencies are distinct and even opposed. But the assumption of an explanatory method which can be taken as *a priori* 'above' all other social experience and cultural production is itself, when analysed, a fact in the sociology of a particular phase of culture. Its modes of privilege, in actual institutions and practices, need especially careful study.

Directions

Cultural sociology, then, is concerned with the social processes of all cultural production, including those forms of production which can be designated as ideologies. This defines a field, but the work now being done, from so many different starting-points, is still a convergence of interests and methods, and there are still crucial theoretical differences at every stage. Another effect of the variety of starting-points, in history, philosophy, literary studies, linguistics, aesthetics and social theory, as well as in sociology itself, is that there is always a problem of overlap with other distinct and still necessary disciplines.

A *sociology* of culture must concern itself with the institutions and formations of cultural production, for this is one of the most distinct of its fields. It is the subject-matter of the second and third chapters of this book. But then a sociology of *culture* must also concern itself with the social relations of its specific means of production. These are the subject of the fourth chapter. It must further concern itself with the ways in which, within social life, 'culture' and 'cultural production' are socially identified and distinguished. These are the subject of the fifth chapter. In all these areas there are overlaps with general history and with the history of particular arts. Cultural sociology cannot replace these, but can put to their material certain distinctively sociological questions.

A sociology of culture must further and most obviously concern itself with specific artistic forms. These, exemplified from drama, are the subject of the sixth chapter. In this area there is overlap with critical analysis and with the general study of sign-systems, as in semiotics. The sociology of cultural forms cannot replace these disciplines, but in its emphasis on the social as well as the notational basis of sign-systems, then seen as general signifying systems, it puts specific sociological questions and adds, to what would otherwise be internal kinds of analysis, a deliberately extended social dimension.

A sociology of culture must further concern itself with the processes of social and cultural 'reproduction'. This is the subject of the seventh chapter. Here there are evident overlaps with political theory and with general sociology, which cultural sociology can not replace but to which it can try to contribute its own kinds of evidence. Finally, a sociology of culture must concern itself with general and specific problems of cultural organization. This is the subject of the eighth chapter. Here there are again overlaps with political theory and with general sociology, which cultural sociology cannot replace but to which it can try to contribute its distinctive emphasis on the organization of signifying systems and on the special kinds of social formation which are professionally concerned with this, among them the difficult category usually identified as 'intellectuals'. In the matter of organization there is also direct overlap with economic analysis, and this is becoming especially important in work on modern capitalist cultural organizations and especially the 'media'. The recent development of a 'political economy of culture' (see Schiller [1969], Murdock and Golding [1974], Garnham [1977]) is especially necessary and welcome, and should be seen as not only distinct from, but complementary to, a cultural sociology.

We have then described a convergence, and the interests and methods which have at once contributed to it and, in most cases, remain important beyond it, as different disciplines. We can now move into the specific areas of its direct concerns.

2 Institutions

Any adequate sociology of culture must, it seems, be an historical sociology. When we look at the vast evidence of the relations of cultural production, in so many different societies and historical periods, it is clear that it would be unwise to adopt, as our first theoretical construct, some universal or general explanatory scheme of the necessary relations between 'culture' and 'society'.

Much actual sociology of culture presumes, in a way inevitably, the typical or dominant relations of the period with which it is concerned; it goes on to adduce detailed evidence of these. But it can then happen that these relations become a norm, from which other periods are interpreted or even, by contrast, judged. The cultural relations of the 'market' are contrasted with those of the 'patron', or the situation of the 'professional artist' with that of the 'State producer'. Many of these terms make sense in a closely defined context, but as we move, with them, towards general sociological statements, they become less and less satisfactory. The important concept of the patron, for example, covers (and then often obscures) at least four or five distinct social relationships in cultural production.

Thus theoretical constructs derived from empirical studies and their extension or generalization are always likely to presume too much, in the transition from local and specific to general concepts. On the other hand, it is only from such studies, at whatever degree of reflection or theoretical remove, that we can begin to shape, test and substantiate our conceptual descriptions. To move, or appear to move, beyond this necessary empirical work, by the early construction of a general theoretical framework, is usually in practice an unargued transition from local and specific to general concepts. Its difference from simple empirical generalization is that whereas this former extends its local names to a variety of historical situations to which they may be only partly appropriate, this latter, theoreticist tendency extends its presumptive interpretations and categories in what is always, essentially, a search for illustrative instances.

Some versions of this tendency are, however, more recognizable as 'theoreticist' than others. The best known example is that of the presumed (theoretical) relationship between 'base' and 'superstructure' in Marxist cultural studies, which in its simplest form asserts that art 'reflects' the socio-economic structure of the society within which it is produced, and then presents its (often persuasive) instances of this relationship. But this kind of Marxist theory should not be isolated. It is in fact no more 'theoreticist' than the basic liberal idea of culture, in which it is presumed that the universal source of cultural production is 'individual expression', so that to study the social relations of cultural activity is to describe the conditions which bear on this norm, permitting or preventing its 'free exercise'. In fact here, as less obviously in the theory of base and superstructure, what is presumed or presented as theory can be seen, on further examination, to be the extension and generalization of the (often very significant) problems, preoccupations and observations of a particular cultural period.

An adequate sociology of culture must work more rigorously. It cannot avoid the informing presence of existing empirical studies and existing theoretical and quasi-theoretical positions. But it must be prepared to rework and reconsider all received material and concepts, and to present its own contributions within the open interaction of evidence and interpretation which is the true condition of its adequacy. All that now follows, in this book, is presented in this sense: as an inquiry and a set of working hypotheses, rather than a body of demonstrated and verified conclusions.

Institutions and formations

We can propose as an initial distinction the following: on the one hand the variable relations between 'cultural producers' (a deliberately neutral if abstract term) and recognizable social *institutions*; on the other hand, the variable relations in which 'cultural producers' have been organized or have organized themselves, their *formations*. This is a working distinction, to make possible some variety of approach to the question of the effective social relations of culture. It is not intended to imply that there are no significant or even causal relations between institutional and formational relationships; indeed, as we shall see, these will often and perhaps always be present. But if we deduce significant cultural relations from the study of institutions alone, we shall be in danger of missing some important cases in which cultural organization has not been, in any ordinary sense, institutional. In particular we may miss the very striking phenomenon of the cultural 'movement', which has been so important in the modern period, and which will be specifically analysed in the next chapter. In the present chapter we shall consider mainly the relations between producers and institutions, and only in that context the question of direct formations.

1 Instituted artists

The first case to consider is that in which, in many relatively early societies, an artist of a certain kind – often in fact a poet – was officially recognized as part of the central social organization itself. This case is so important, by comparison with the social situations of artists in later societies, that it is often presented as if it were singular and uniform, and this can have important effects on its more general interpretation. Where we have records of such official recognition within the central social organization, we find not only – as we might expect – differences between different societies but also historical differences, between different forms of a continuing society. This is very clear, for all the uncertainty of detail, in the characteristic case of the Celtic bards.

Thus we can say that in traditional Celtic societies the bard was given an honoured place in the official organization of the 'kingdom' or 'tribe'. But the real social relations were always more complex and variable. The earliest evidence we have, from observation by the Romans of the the Celts in Gaul, is already from a considerably developed society. What this evidence suggests is a particular stage in the specialization of functions which, at still earlier stages, would – as in many comparable cases – not have been clearly distinguished. This process of specialization is of course central to cultural history (see Chapter 5). The functions which can later be distinguished as those of 'priest', 'prophet' or 'bard' – and in more modern terms 'historian' or even 'scientist' – were often originally exercised by the same individuals or groups of individuals. The distinction of these functions was in part a result of their internal development, as each function required more skill and time. But it was also, and perhaps primarily, a result of more general changes in social organization and in the mode of production. At any rate, by the time we can observe such changes, the 'official recognition' turns out to be an element of a structured aristocratic society.

Thus it is said (though still with problems of interpretation) that the bards were a specific order ranking below the priests and the seers, though composing with them a specific privileged caste. There is then an immediate problem in interpreting their actual social relations. It has been said, on the one hand, that in this situation the bard is accountable to society, and is its spokesman; on the other hand, that it is his duty to serve the past and present glory of the ruling class. By the time we come, at a later stage again, to any evidence of actual work, we can certainly see the fulfilment of the latter function, in the very common eulogy or encomium of men in power. But then, extending from these, we can see the mixed character of the sagas and genealogies, which often function as legitimation of power but are also versions of history. Beyond these again, there are clear cases of more general lore and precept and observation, which undoubtedly served a more extended social function. Moreover there is evidence of some relative independence even in relation to direct rulers, as in the conflicts and subsequent laws, in Irish literature, about the use of the lampoon. Or again: 'the bards of the world pass judgement on men of valour,' as a sixth-century Welsh poet (Aneirin) wrote, in a remarkable poem mourning a defeat and honouring those who died in it.

The recognition and further specialization of the bardic function continued to change, as the societies changed. Thus after the Christianization of Ireland, the priestly function was removed to a quite different kind of order, increasingly employing writing, while the bardic function, still often oral, entered a different and more specialized relationship to the aristocratic families. In Welsh literature, by the tenth century, the official status of bards was codified in grades: the chief poet, the battle poet, the minstrel; with assigned differences of subject and in some respects of audience, and with relatively strict internal rules about the craft itself. As society changed further, and especially as the political independence of the courts within which the poets worked was weakened and finally lost, the social relations changed again, and the literary organization became at once more specialized and more socially disconnected.

This is the point at which, for all the relatively doubtful and overlapping cases, we can mark a change from one category of social relations to another. After the very earliest period of relative non-differentiation of functions, in which the 'literary' or 'artistic' had not or not fully separated out from the more generally 'cultural', there had been this phase of *specifically instituted artists*, which should not really be described in terms taken from later phases, such as 'official recognition' or 'patronage'. Each of these later terms implies an act of variable social choice: *deciding* to recognize a poet or poets; *deciding* to act as patron to them. But in this important early phase, the social position of this kind of cultural producer was instituted as such, and as an integral part of general social organization. We have still to remember its variations, in the changing periods and structures of such societies, but as a categorical distinction it is reasonably clear.

2 Artists and patrons

The distinction that matters is from that of 'patronage', which itself, as we shall see, is highly varied.

(i) From institution to patronage

There is one early form of patronage which is in effect a modulation of the earlier situation of the instituted artist, in altered social conditions. The change is marked, for example, in Welsh literature by the transition from the instituted court poets (the 'poets of the princes') to the 'poets of the nobility' who were now, though still highly regarded, more *occasionally* dependent. A poet might be attached to a household, or, increasingly, be dependent on travelling between households, performing his work and looking for hospitality and support.

This is the beginning of a transition from the social relations of a regular institution (its exchange factors fully integrated and in that sense coherent) to the social relations of conscious exchange, though of course not yet of full exchange. It was part of the social self-definition of the patronizing household, often deliberately in terms residual from the true courts, to assume what was at once a responsibility and an honour. Meanwhile, the specific literary organization – the residual bardic order – was to an important extent self-defining in shared grades and rules.

(ii) Retainer and commission

A second and much more general form of patronage was that of a court or powerful household in which there was no intrinsic organization of artists as part of the general social organization but in which, often very extensively, individual artists were retained, often with titles which represent the true cases of 'official recognition'. In painting and music, especially, this kind of patronage was extremely important and lasted for many centuries. Its detailed arrangements varied, in the many thousands of cases, but what is generally true about its form of social relations is that the artist was typically retained or commissioned as an individual professional worker. This is a crucial stage of development from that in which – in the earlier stages substantially, in the later stages residually – artists were themselves a specific form of social organization. At the same time, under the general conditions of this best-known of all forms of patronage, certain less specific forms of professional organization in the arts were often present, at a different stage: evidently in the master and apprentice system which was at times similar to that in a wider area of skills and crafts (see pages 58ff below).

The distinction can be interestingly explored in relation to the very large amount of art – painting, sculpture, architecture, music and (in a different sense) literature – produced within the variable social relations of the Christian church. Some of the best-known work of this kind is at least analogous to that of court patronage; the large amount of art commissioned by the Vatican Court is an obvious example. Yet there is also a less determinate area, in which artists devoted themselves to religious art not only, and sometimes not primarily, because this was the willed commission of their immediate patron, but because they could identify themselves with the religious purpose of which the immediate social organization was the available manifest form. This willing integration is significantly different from the case at the other end of this spectrum, where the individual artist is in effect available for hire to glorify or embellish the particular court or household which has hired him. For while the immediate economic relations were often similar, as the specific form of patronal exchange, the full social relations can be seen as variable, once the fact of willing and independent service of a social and religious kind is admitted.

Indeed, there had been, within the Church, a relation more analogous to that of the instituted artists of earlier social orders. In the monasteries, especially, we can find many interesting cases of specific forms of organization which, while governed by manifest religious rather than secular rules (and in that sense relatively displaced from the integration of such an organization in the direct social organization as a whole), functioned in practice as cultural organizations, of great significance, in learning, in literature, in dramatic writing and in the visual arts. Since the order was primarily religious it has to be distinguished from specific cultural orders, but it is even more distinct from the social relations of patronage. Within such an order, many producers became in effect specialists, yet still within the terms of a general organization beyond their specialism. The transition to full ecclesiastical patronage – a transition of course marked by many intermediate and overlapping stages – was a transition to those forms of professionalism, involving mobility and availability for hire, which are characteristic of the second main form of patronage.

(iii) Protection and support

The third form of patronage is again distinct, in that it is concerned less with the direct retaining and commissioning of artists than with the provision of some kind of social protection or recognition. The theatrical companies of Elizabethan England are good examples of this kind. There might still be some direct commissioning, and some direct (retaining) support, but the main function of such patronage was social support, in the uncertain social and legal conditions of theatres and actors. This relatively explicit form can be seen to modulate into the process of association of particular works with particular powerful names: the patron, in effect, as dedicatee. This was a milder form of social support, moving towards mere social recommendation. It often did not involve economic exchange relations. What was really being exchanged, within a specific kind of society marked by overt class inequalities, was a hopefully mutual reputation and honour

(iv) Sponsorship

It is then necessary to distinguish this type of patronage from a fourth kind, in a period in which there were qualitatively new social relations of art, determined by the increasingly regular production of works of art as commodities for general sale. In either form there were continuities from earlier forms of patronage, but now in more complex and more open societies. The patrons of the first and second kinds offered hospitality, reward and (in some cases of the second kind) direct monetary exchange, but for work then specifically performed for and (where relevant) owned by them. The patron of the third kind, offering social reputation and protection, often worked within conditions where the work was being partly or wholly offered to a paying public; the Elizabethan public theatres were in that sense fully commercial institutions. The patron of the fourth kind, though continuing some of the earlier functions, worked more fully within a world in which the production of works of art for sale was normal. His function was to provide early support, or early encouragement, to artists beginning to make their way in the market, or unable to sustain some particular project within it. The typical relation was monetary, and it came to be generalized from the individual patron to the eighteenth-century form of subscription-list (pre-publication). But there was still a residue of the functions of social reputation and recommendation.

Commercial sponsorship. This fourth form of patronage survived into conditions in which commodity and market relations had become dominant. Indeed it can still be found in our own time, in some individual cases but also in new forms of patronage. There is a limited sense in which some industrial and commercial corporations have entered into patronage of the second kind, analogous to earlier courts and households, commissioning works for their own use or ownership. But while some of these cases are of this simple kind, others are more directly involved with modern market conditions, whether as a form of investment or as a form of prestige advertising.

(v) The public as 'patron'

Public 'patronage', from revenues raised by taxation, has some continuities of function and attitude with earlier forms, but some quite new definitions of function, such as the deliberate maintenance and extension of the arts as a matter of general public policy. Many of the controversies about the new institutions which serve these purposes can be seen, on analysis, to be arguments about different forms of patronage – encouragement or intervention within and beyond the market – but also, and crucially, about distinctions between the social relations of patronage (where the public body is held merely to have replaced the court or the household or the individual patron) and the alternative social relations of a now publicly instituted art.

The most available historical models are all from the period of different forms of patronage, and it is not surprising that these have been predominant in the forms of new public bodies. Yet there is considerable tension between such models and the fact of public revenue. The historical models of instituted or integrated arts, as distinct from patronized arts, are mostly too far back, in such evidently different social orders, for the principles under-lying them to be easy to grasp. Yet the defining charac-teristic of all patronal social relations is the privileged situation of the patron. Within varying forms of self-definition of the honours or responsibilities that go with such privilege, the patron is defined as one who can give or withhold his commission or support. The specific social relations of such privilege are of course derived from the social order as a whole; it is there that the patron's powers and resources are enrolled or protected; in the crudest terms, he is doing what he wishes with his own. It is this fact, above all, which makes the patronal definition of any public body, deriving its authority and resources from the supposed general will of the society, at best controversial, at worst quite inapplicable. Yet the habituated relations of various forms of patronage, and of artists as 'clients', have in practice persisted into these otherwise new forms.

3 Artists and markets

Historically there is a long period of overlap between patronal and market social relations in the arts. Yet in principle they can be readily distinguished. Production for the market involves the conception of the work of art as a commodity, and of the artist, however else he may define himself, as a particular kind of commodity producer. But there are then crucially different phases of commodity production. All involve production for simple monetary exchange; the work is offered for sale and is bought and thus owned. But the social relations of artists involved partly or wholly in commodity production are in fact highly variable.

(i) Artisanal

There is the simple, early but in some areas persistent situation of the independent producer who offers his own work for direct sale. This is usually called *artisanal*. The producer is wholly dependent on the immediate market, but within its terms his work remains under his own direction, at all stages, and he can see himself, in this sense, as independent.

(ii) Post-artisanal

The next phase of commodity production is very different, but itself has two stages. First, the producer sells his work not directly but to a *distributive* intermediary, who then becomes, in a majority of cases, his factual if often occasional employer. Then, second, the producer sells his work to a *productive* intermediary, and typically capitalist social relations begin to be instituted. The intermediary invests in the purchase of a work for the purpose of profit; it is now *his* relations with the market which are direct.

We can see the complex relations of this crucial *post-artisanal* phase in, for example, the evolution of booksellers into publishers. The phase is typically characterized by the outright purchase of the works in question. In much of his immediate situation, the producer remains an artisan, but now in a more complex and more organized market in which he is practically dependent on intermediaries. It is worth emphasizing that there can be significant variations, within this situation, in the productive process itself. At one level, the producer is still offering his own product, work completed before the offer for sale. But to the extent that such relations become normal or, in certain areas, dominant, he can in the end, basically, be offering his labour, to produce works of a certain known type.

There is great practical complexity in the various stages of transition between these essentially alternative relationships. This is true also of that other level, at which the producer defines, to himself, the nature of his work. This is the source of the many important and difficult arguments about the relations between the artist's responsibility to his work and his 'responsibility', or 'obligation', or 'subjection' to a 'public' and to a 'market'. Some of these arguments substantially repeat earlier arguments about the relations between an artist and his patron, but others, within the expansion, diffusion and relative displacement of the artist's social relations in this sense, are qualitatively new. It is significant, for example, that the artist's claim to 'freedom', to 'create as he wishes', was much more commonly made after the institution of dominant market relations, and must be both positively and negatively related to them.

Neither the artisanal nor the post-artisanal phase of market relations in cultural production can be said to have ended. Indeed the phases seem to be variable between specific arts. Thus in painting, where patronal relations, in directly commissioned works (the simplest example is the portrait), have also persisted, there are still some examples of artisanal and many post-artisanal relations, the latter still often in their first phase, where a painter's relations to a gallery which sells his work are still commonly in the distributive phase. In music, where there are still also patronal relations in commissioned works, there are still predominantly distributive post-artisanal relations in orchestral works and in traditional sheet music, while in popular music the second, productive post-artisanal phase has long been established, and there has been major movement into later phases of market relations. In literature, though there are still cases of artisanal and distributive post-artisanal relations, productive post-artisanal relations have long been dominant, and important internal changes within them have taken much publishing into a later market phase.

These variations between arts are important in themselves and also as a reminder that the social relations of artists are closely related to the technical means of production of each specific art. The general question of the relational effects of these means of production is discussed in Chapter 4, but some of their institutional effects are noted here as they occur.

(iii) Market professional

The internal changes in productive post-artisanal relations in literature are especially significant in understanding the next market phase. They are very complex in effect, since there is both increasing capitalization of the productive intermediaries – modern publishers – and increasing professionalization, of a specific kind, among writers. The two significant indicators of these changing relations are *copyright* and *royalty*.

In this period of cultural technology, and especially in the nineteenth century, the reproducibility of print was very much ahead of most other kinds of artistic reproduction, and this made the question of property in the work acute. A writer's productive (post-artisanal) relations with a publisher could be, and widely were, bypassed, by other publishers (domestic 'pirates' or foreigners) who reprinted and sold the work without reference or relation to the author. A long struggle by writers to establish first domestic and then international copyright resulted not only in a new concept of literary property but new, or at least amended, social relationships of writers. For although works were still passed to productive intermediaries, their general ownership tended to remain in the producer's hands The newly typical relationship was a negotiated contract for a specific form or period of publication, with variable clauses on its terms and duration. As an expression of this relationship, the 'royalty' – a specific payment on each copy of this form sold – came to replace the common earlier form of outright purchase.

Thus the writer became a participant in the direct market process of the sale of his work. The terms of this participation have been endlessly argued about, and the increasing practice of the advance on royalties has to some extent modified it, in restoring an element of purchase. But the general result, for all its great unevenness between writers, was a specific kind of social relationship which can be defined as a form of professional independence within integrated and dominant market relations. Typically, writers became involved in relations with the market as a whole, rather than with a specific productive intermediary, and this generalization of full market relations took them, in majority, beyond the post-artisanal phase and into the phase of the organized professional market. Further intermediaries, such as literary agencies, marked this more developed phase.

Perception of the 'market'. In all these market phases, the producer could still be seen as an originator, though in practice, throughout, there were qualifications. The artisan, the post-artisan in indirect distributive or productive relations and the market professional all attended necessarily, at some point, though in remarkably varying degrees, to that form of demand or projected demand which was mediated, with increasing indirectness, by the form of the actual selling relationship. Indeed production *for* the market, as a purpose taking priority over any other, is widely evident in each phase, though there are many examples of producers struggling against or effectively ignoring market trends. Culturally this interaction is crucial, for it defines the social relations of artists at a different level from that of most other kinds of production. Characteristically it becomes difficult, but also necessary, in just this market phase, to distinguish this form of production from others with which it had analogous economic relations. Our conventional distinctions between 'artisan', 'craftsman' and 'artist' belong to this phase of the cultural market, but as responses to its internal difficulties.

At the root of these distinctions is an attempted differentiation between the production of one kind of object and another. This can be expressed as a contrast between the 'merely utilitarian' and the 'artistic', or, on the other hand, between the 'useful' and the 'merely cultural'. There can be no doubt that over the whole range covered by these attempted distinctions there are substantial differences of immediacy and perception of use and need. It can indeed be argued that this has always been so, in pre-market as in market conditions. We can construct a plausible hierarchy of material and cultural needs in which the cooking-pot or the shoe will always be more 'needed', and in that sense more 'useful', than the painting or the story or song. But the most effective way of exploring this difficult question is not in abstract, supra-historical terms. It is in examining the ways in which these problems of need and use are practically organized, in specific social orders.

What we then see is that the hierarchy of use and need is itself directly related to the character of the organizing productive relations. Where it was necessary, for example, to make art-objects as a form of delineation of the governing kinship relations, or a form of practical relations with the natural world, or – as so often – as a form of the reproduction of a specific social or social-metaphysical order, the problem of hierarchy is radically different from the outset. Indeed it is well known that societies which were very poor, by all later standards, allotted very significant time, energy and resources to the production of what would now be distinguished as art-objects. In all the later, more organized phases of this type, at a time when the practice of art had been both distinguished and specialized, the institution of artists as part of the general social organization was still, as we have seen, normal.

The exceptional difficulty of the place of 'cultural' production in modern societies can then in its turn be examined in terms of its relations to the general productive order. And here there is at once a difficulty, in that the general productive order, throughout the centuries of the development of capitalism, has been predominantly defined by the market, and 'cultural production', as we have seen, has been increasingly assimilated to its terms, yet any full identity between cultural production and general production has been to an important extent resisted, one of the forms of this resistance being the distinctions between 'artisan', 'craftsman' and 'artist', and in an important related form the distinction between 'objects of utility' and 'objects of art'. Thus it would be true to say that the source of these modern difficulties is indeed the market economy, but on the other hand, on the evidence of the attempts at distinctions, it would not be true – it would in fact be seriously reductive – to say that the general market order has transformed all cultural production into a market-commodity type.

For while the earlier forms of patronal relations are in general residual from more culturally integrated societies, many of the later forms are precisely interventions either within, or at times against and beyond, normal market forces. We are then faced, not for the first time in the analysis of societies economically based on capitalist modes of production, with certain significant asymmetries between the social relations of the dominant productive mode and other relations within the general social and cultural order.

These should not be exaggerated. Most relations of cultural production have indeed been assimilated to the terms of the developing market. But some have not, and it is significant that these are defended in terms of types of production which are important 'in and for themselves'. On this basis they are distinguished from 'production' by the difficult specialization of 'creative activities'.

At the level of definitions, this has never been satisfactory. The widespread and in many cases willing and eager involvement of cultural producers in what are really quite normal market relationships has always cut across it. But this has significantly led, within each art, to further attempted distinctions between 'commercial' and other ('creative', 'authentic') forms of the same manifest practice. And while we should never pretend that the distinctions are adequate, in their usually rather complacent conventional forms, it would be quite wrong to disregard the actual or attempted social relations, of an alternative kind, which the attempts at differentiation, and the initiatives and marginal institutions corresponding to them, undoubtedly represent.

(iv) Corporate professional

The question has become more acute in the latest phase of market relations, which is that of the corporate. This phase is mainly associated with very important developments in the means of cultural production, and especially the use of new media. But in one or two areas the corporate development is not wholly related to these. In writing, for example, the field of market relations was affected by new kinds of combine and corporate development in magazine and newspaper publishing. Social relations typical of the integrated professional market persisted into this phase, but there was also a significant development of new social relations, for some kinds of writer, who were now effectively or wholly employed within the new corporate structures. This tendency has steadily increased, and alongside it there has been a different but related tendency, as combine and corporate ownership have become much more common in book publishing. Again, here, the social relationships of the professional market have persisted, but there has been a significant and growing development of some new relations, within an increasingly capitalized corporate sector.

These relations turn on the question of the origin of production. In some earlier relations, notably those of the productive post-artisanal and the market professional, it indeed quite often happened that a work originated in a commission, from a bookseller or publisher. But in the corporate structure this has become very much more common, in relation to a highly organized and fully capitalized market in which the direct commissioning of planned saleable products has become a normal mode.

It is virtually impossible to estimate the proportion of such relations, within books as a whole, since some and perhaps much commissioning is still, in cultural terms, governed by considerations of what authors would in any case have wished to write. But in an important and rising number of cases, the relations are not really of this kind. The dominance of the corporate publishing sector is such that for many writers the most available social relations are those of employment in this sense, with the ideas for books coming from new professional intermediaries (publishers' editors) within the market structure, and authors being employed to execute them.

Relations then vary from diverse occasional employment, still not far from the situation of the market professional, to quite new relations, through retainers and serial contracts, in which the writer becomes, in effect, the employed and (with modifications such as royalties) salaried professional.

New media. But of course the most important cases of the rise of the salaried professional in cultural production have occurred in the institutions of the new media, in which integrated social production became normal and necessary. Cinema, radio and television are the outstanding examples, in which capitalist and some non-capitalist corporations organize production from the beginning and offer salaried or contracted employment within these terms. The great cultural importance of these new media has made these social relations, in the late twentieth century, dominant and even typical.

There is then a qualitative change from earlier socio-cultural relations, even within the earlier market phases. For the effective (if of course never absolute) origin of cultural production is now centrally sited within the corporate market. The scale of capital involved, and the dependence on more complex and specialized means of production and distribution, have to an important extent blocked access to these media in older artisanal, post-artisanal and even market professional terms, and imposed predominant conditions of corporate employment.

This does not mean, of course, that older forms of relation have not survived elsewhere. In the older arts of painting and sculpture, orchestral music and, as we have seen, some writing, the complex relations of the individual producer (and originator) have persisted. But in music, for example, these older relations have become minor by comparison with the new corporate institutions of popular music, based on the new technologies of disc and cassette, where the corporate capitalist mode is decisive.

Advertising. We should note also a form of cultural production which is highly specific to the phase of the corporate market: what is still called 'advertising'. In earlier phases of a market society some advertising, usually specific or classified, existed in the margins of other cultural institutions, and drew on some general cultural skills. But from the period of corporate organization, beginning in the press in the late nineteenth century, it became, in specific ways, a form of cultural production in itself. Advertising agencies which had begun by booking insertions became, in the twentieth century, institutions of a form of cultural production, wholly governed by the organized market. It is interesting that producers within advertising agencies were quick to claim the title 'creative'. By the late twentieth century, with the increasing dependence of many other cultural institutions on revenue or sponsorship from this specific market institution, 'advertising' had become a quite new cultural phenomenon and was characteristically being extended into areas of social, economic and explicitly political values, as a new kind of corporate cultural institution.

Thus the late phases of a market culture are very different from its early phases. Its institutions, in their increasing centrality, have moved towards a situation in which it could again be said (but with the qualitative difference of an epochal change) that cultural institutions are integral parts of the general social organization. In a modern capitalist economy, and its characteristic kind of social order, the cultural institutions of press and publishing, cinema, radio, television and the record industry, are no longer, as in earlier market phases, marginal or minor, but, both in themselves and in their frequent interlock or integration with other productive institutions, are parts of the whole social and economic organization at its most general and pervasive.

4 Post-market institutions

Yet modern cultural institutions cannot be understood exclusively in terms of the corporate market and the persistence of some earlier market forms. Three kinds of post-market institutions have become important; they can be distinguished as the modern patronal, the intermediate and the governmental. Their incidence varies within different societies at comparable stages of general development.

Modern patronal and intermediate
The modern patronal is common in advanced capitalist societies. Certain arts which are not profitable or even viable in market terms are sustained by specific institutions such as foundations, by organizations of subscribers, and still by some private patronage. Intermediate between this and full governmental institutions are bodies wholly or significantly financed from the public revenue (as in Great Britain the Arts Council) which fund certain arts. Or in the same general category there are institutions like some of those in broadcasting (in Great Britain the BBC) which depend on one form or another of public revenue but which direct their own production. Social relations of producers to the modern patronal and intermediate institutions range from the patronal, through the post-artisanal and professional, to (as in most broadcasting) corporate employment.

Governmental
In some capitalist societies, and in most post-capitalist societies, cultural institutions have become departments of state, especially in the modern media. There is a variety of detailed arrangements, but the typical relations of producers in these conditions are those of state-corporate employees, or in some cases state rather than market professionals. Conditions then vary from those in which the cultural institutions and their producers are wholly subordinated to general state policy – a condition often made harsher by full or attempted monopoly of all means of cultural production – to more nuanced situations in which, while general policy direction is exercised, the practical

relations are not significantly different from those in modern patronal and intermediate bodies, which of course also, in varying ways, have general policy directions in accordance with the social order in which they are working.

Conclusion

The sociology of culture, at this level of institutions, has then to take account of both historical and contemporary diversity. It is important to retain the full range of provisional classification of institutions and types of relations, as the means to specific analysis, rather than to work with the (pre-sociological) formulas of 'the artist' and 'his public', or 'the cultural superstructure' and 'the economic base'. Indeed it is at once the changing social history and the complex sociology of the changing institutions and relations which take us beyond these formulas to the possibility of more precise analysis

3 Formations

In much work in the sociology of culture, we find that we have to deal not only with general institutions and their typical relations, but also with forms of organization and self-organization which seem much closer to cultural production.

1 Early forms of internal organization

We have already noticed some early examples of this, in such cases as the internal organization of the bardic orders, which were concerned not only with social position and relations, but with the practice (at several stages, the rules) of the art itself. However strange this may seem within the modern formula of the artist as free creative individual, there can be no real doubt that major art, of certain kinds, was produced and sustained in these ways. There is a direct relation, of course, between this strict form of internal organization and the integration of its order within the general social order. Significant breaks from the rules, or the opposite cases of their increasing formalization and rigidity, can often be related to periods of change or crisis in this general relationship.

Bardic rules

Thus it was in the period of the Welsh court poets (the *Gogynfeirdd*), at a time of severe political crisis under the encroachments of English power in the twelfth and thirteenth centuries, that the strictest regulation and formalization (in most people's opinion, also, the isolation and specialization) of the rules of poetic composition can be found. A decisive break from the narrowness of these rules came in the fourteenth century, with Dafydd ap Gwilym, in a period marked both by increasing interaction with a more general European culture, after the loss of political independence, and yet, creatively, by a new 'national' poetry, itself governed by more flexible but still clear internal rules (the *cywydd* metre). The internal social organization of the poets changed in the same period as this specific artistic change.

Guilds

An important and different form of internal organization, distinct from at least the main phases of the bardic orders, is the *craft guild*, which was very common in later medieval society. This marked a shift from the integrated singular order within which the bardic and similar orders were first defined, though in its disputed origins the guild may once have been close to them. By the time we have adequate records, the craft guild can be seen emerging from the *lodge* of craftsmen working together on a project. It became at once more general and more regulated. In an increasingly mercantile society, the craft guild served a variety of functions, social, religious and economic. Some of its most significant early relations were with the *guild merchant*, which sought to regulate the conditions of urban trade.

The craft guild, or 'mistery' or 'company', organized the artisans of a particular craft, and in most cases provided specifically for craft training and for the maintenance of craft standards. In the case of what we would now distinguish as 'arts', an early example is the fourteenth-century Florentine guild, actually that of the surgeon apothecaries but including painters from an overlap of working materials. A special branch for artists, with compulsory membership, was formed in 1360. In addition to this kind of specific organization, guilds in some societies were involved in more general cultural production. The most important example in England is that of the urban dramatic festivals, of cycles of religious 'mystery' plays, where responsibility for production was distributed among the craft guilds.

In changing conditions of trade, the self-management of many of the early guilds gave way to restrictive and eventually unacceptable forms of internal dominance and privilege. The master-apprentice system, which was always inherent, developed from a craft emphasis to what was in the end an unmistakeable class emphasis, with new restrictions, privileges and financial qualifications attached to mastership. There were attempted revivals of the earlier spirit, as in the *compagnonnage* movement of self-organizing journeymen. But in the case of most crafts there was a long and complex development towards the radically different organization of the craft or trade *union*, which belongs to the epoch of predominantly capitalist development and social relations. Even along this road, however, many of the old 'guilds' had become, in effect, the organizations of employing 'masters' – the craft status shifted to the economic status – and these were themselves in complex relations with the development of capitalist trade, which was breaking down the kind of autonomy from which the guilds, new and old, had derived their monopoly.

Academies

In the case of what we now call 'the arts', and above all in painting and sculpture, a different form of organization developed, in the *academy*. This emergence marks two shifts: first, the declining importance of the church as the main patron for art, which produced a more secular emphasis – the guilds, it will be remembered, had almost always included a specifically religious element; and, second, an increasing differentiation of 'arts' from 'crafts'.

The earlier specification of the 'liberal arts' had been primarily of branches of knowledge. The usual list was grammar, rhetoric and dialectic; music, arithmetic, geometry and astronomy – where only music and some elements of grammar and rhetoric would now be recognized as 'arts'. The shift among painters and sculptors, who had been in the craft guilds, is most clearly marked in the adoption of the term 'academy' from the place of the famous school of Plato. This had already been widely adopted as the name of a higher school. This specifically educational definition has of course continued, but its adoption by artists marks a significant shift. On the one hand it led to the concept of art education rather than craft training, with the professor-student relationship substituted for that of the master-apprentice. On the other hand, it marked the new and broadly secular movement towards the independent status of 'arts and learning'; indeed, though the term is not yet used, of 'culture'.

As a result of these two tendencies, the academy, historically, had a range of functions and was often internally diverse. Thus there was an academy of practising poets in Toulouse in the early fourteenth century. There was an informal academy of painters and sculptors, attended by Michelangelo, in Florence at the turn from the fifteenth to the sixteenth century. There was the later, more famous and (under ducal patronage) more recognized,

Accademia del Disegno of Vasari, from 1563. Many subsequent academies of this kind were founded, usually with an increasingly formal organization of instruction. But also, from its early stages, the academy could be either a general or, increasingly, a specialized learned society; there are many such examples, from the thirteenth century onwards, in speculative philosophy, literature and language, and the sciences.

Exhibitions

The subsequent development of academies is then very complex. One direct line is the emergence from the art-teaching academies of the annual exhibition, begun in Paris in 1667 and widely imitated throughout Europe. This eventually set a pattern of official exhibition, from which, as we shall see, there were many crucial later breaks. But this type of development was more evident in the centralized royal states. In other societies – for example, the Netherlands – forms of guild organization persisted, and artists worked for the market through the new intermediaries, the dealers.

Cultural effects of academies

Where the academies were powerful, there was a complex overlap between social position and artistic prestige. By the mid-eighteenth century there were powerful complaints against their authority, both in general social terms and because of their embodiment of 'academicism' in art: the teaching of principles and rules which, it was argued, worked against the practice of original art. This situation and its controversies have continued, but in general, from the eighteenth century, increasingly specialized academies came through as institutions for teaching many of the arts. The learned and scientific academies took in general a different course, since education in their disciplines was predominantly centred in the universities.

Professional societies

Meanwhile, alongside the later phases of the academy, there was an important new phase of internal cultural organization, corresponding to the emergence of the market professional. The new type of 'professional society' was founded primarily to regulate the new economic arrangements. There is a typical example among writers, seeking to protect copyright and to negotiate general contract conditions. By the twentieth century many of these were beginning to move, through much internal controversy about the social-class implications, to a kind of trade-union status and function. This movement has been especially evident under the pressure of economic conditions in an increasingly corporate market.

But then it is characteristic of this latest phase that the professional society is primarily a *business* organization. This highlights the fact that there had been a practical separation between the organizations of business and artistic concerns, which in earlier types of organization had often seemed to be, and in many cases clearly were, united.

'Movements'

It is at this point that we need to introduce the concept of a quite different type of cultural formation, in which artists come together in the common pursuit of some specific artistic aim. Such formations, under the names of 'movement', 'school', 'circle' and so on, or under the taken or given label of a specific 'ism', are so important in cultural history, and especially modern cultural history, that they present a special, difficult, yet unavoidable problem in social analysis. What then are these specific artistic formations?

2 Movements as formations

The initial problem is in the terms themselves, since some of the most common descriptions of relatively informal groups, notably 'school', have been shared, often by deliberate if critical imitation, with more formal institutions. Yet this complexity of terms does no more than represent, indeed often under-represent, the complexity of the actual history.

'Schools'
Thus a 'school' can be literally that, in its modern sense: an institution in which there are a master and pupils, whose characteristic work can be identified. This is one main use in, for example, descriptions of tendencies in classical Greek philosophy. But the term was also available for broader or more informal tendencies. The original Greek word had passed from meaning 'leisure' to the 'employment of leisure in disputation' and from that to both the institutional meaning and the more general description of a tendency. Thus a 'school' can be a general tendency, often identified by the name of a particular 'master', who need not, however, be in direct institutional or even otherwise direct relations with his 'pupils' or 'disciples'.

But also, broadening the other way, a 'school' can be a whole body of teachers of a discipline, in a particular place, and then by no means necessarily a specific tendency or body of doctrine. In universities, where the term became common for the body of teachers of a subject, there are examples both of the specifying tendency and of the neutral institutional description. In painting in Renaissance Italy, where the term 'school' is now commonly used in classification, the crux of the definition is usually a particular city – Florence or Venice – within which certain identifiable styles and techniques were developed, sometimes by direct teaching, at other times by the more general facts of civic association and mutual influence.

In this range of senses, we find forms of association of artists which have continued to be important. Moreover, beyond the identifiable forms of actual association, an additional emphasis has been given by the methodology of most forms of cultural historiography, which distinguish and classify 'schools' or more general 'movements' and 'tendencies'. It is clear that this can have no retrospective effect on the actual forms of association, but it can have important other effects, since in presenting the history of philosophy or painting in this way it suggests forms of identification or association to new contributors. Yet while there is both an actual continuity of forms and this kind of imputed or suggested continuity, it is clear that there are also new social forms and variations of received forms. Some of these can be directly related to changes in the general social relations of cultural production.

'Independents'

The case of new organizations of painters is particularly instructive. The vast number of self-instituted independent organizations in the nineteenth century, and into the twentieth century, can in many cases be directly related to two related factors: the development of the teaching academy, with its tendency to prescribe rules; and the greatly increased importance of the exhibition, within the market conditions which had succeeded patronage.

Breakaway groups

We can attach variable importance to either factor, in each

individual case, but in their outcome they are often inextricably fused. While the academies monopolized exhibitions, there would always be arguments about selection and the principles of selection. Thus the breakaway group, organizing its own exhibition, was an obvious initiative. There are very many such cases, the most famous being the *Salon des Refusés*, of 1863, at which Manet, Pissarro and Cézanne exhibited. In this case much of the work shown was subsequently (and through this emphasis) identified as an autonomous stylistic movement in art, and of course this was often likely to be the case. It is so in the famous *Sezession* in Vienna in 1897, in relation to *art nouveau*, and *Die Brücke*, from 1905, in relation to expressionism.

Specializing groups

On the other hand there are cases, such as the English Free Society of Artists, in the late eighteenth century, in which the fact of independent exhibition was more important than any actual innovation in style. There are also many cases in which the break was mainly functional, within the general practice, to give emphasis to, or to redress academic neglect of, engravers, watercolourists and so on. In yet other cases, such as the early-nineteenth-century German Brotherhood of St Luke, the emphasis was on the breakaway from academic training towards a workshop kind of organization, more centred on training and development than on exhibition.

Types of group organization

The sociology of such groups is already complex, but it is important that in most cases in this phase some kind of organization was instituted; indeed there were often constitutional rules. The cases in which there was no constitution, or lesser formality of organization, merge into

types of association which are more characteristic of the
twentieth century (though some of the earlier forms have
continued). Here the break is more explicitly towards a
particular style or more general cultural position. It may
include such devices as collective exhibition or similar
public manifestations, but it often does not include actual
membership of anything. It is a looser form of group
association, primarily defined by shared theory and
practice, and its immediate social relations are often not
easy to distinguish from those of a group of friends who
share common interests.

The sociology of such groups, internally considered, is
then obviously difficult, in any orthodox terms. Yet a
general sociology of the phase in which the formation of
such groups can be seen as culturally distinctive, alongside
more formal and established organizations, is at once
necessary and fascinating.

3 Some principles of independent formations

It is obviously easier to offer social analysis of a formal
institution, with its regularized type of internal organization, and its commonly regulated relations to the rest of
society, than even to begin analysis of the relatively
informal associations which have been so important in
modern cultural life.

There are particular methodological difficulties, beyond
the level of relative formality or informality. Such cultural
groups are typically small in numbers, and offer little
opportunity for reliable statistical analysis, of the kind
which is normal for larger institutions and groups. This is
why, among other reasons, orthodox sociology has found it
(apparently) easier to analyse cultural effects, where large
numbers and control groups are available, than to analyse

the social relations of cultural production. Indeed this emphasis has persisted into a period where, in the new media, large-scale organizations are in fact available for analysis. It might then be tempting to pass straight to this later type of analysis, of the newspaper office, the publishing combine, the broadcasting company, the film corporation; indeed such work is necessary. But while there has been little analysis of the social relations of earlier, equally formal though smaller, or less formal and indeed informal institutions and associations, there ought to be some theoretical hesitation.

For it is characteristic of the social relations of any cultural production that there is a problem about the definition of the purpose of any particular organization. The distinction must not be too sharply drawn; similar problems occur in the analysis of educational or religious organizations. But there is usually an effective distinction from the institutions of simple commodity production – even where the cultural work is quite clearly a commodity it is almost always, and often justly, also described in very different terms – and from the institutions or power and administration, in which purposes and objectives are inherent. As we distinguish this specific character of cultural production we should hesitate before attempting sociological analysis of modern cultural corporations, which in other respects resemble contemporary large-scale manufacturing and administrative organizations. Certain principles of analysis have to be learned in work on other types of cultural formation, and on the relations between formal and informal, established and breakaway formations, before the problems which are being negotiated and at times overridden in the combines and corporations can be substantively rather than merely organizationally assessed (see pages 116ff below).

Yet the difficulties of method then return. To the

relatively small numbers involved in many cultural
organizations and associations we must add the characteristic of relatively short, often extremely short, duration.
Among the relatively or wholly informal groups and
associations, the rapidity of formation and dissolution, the
complexity of internal breaks and of fusions, can seem quite
bewildering. Yet this is no reason for ignoring what, taken
as a whole process, is so general a social fact.

Types of modern cultural formation

In full awareness of these difficulties, some principles of an
appropriate kind of analysis can be suggested and briefly
exemplified. Thus it is an evident advance on a mere
empirical listing of successive 'movements' or 'isms',
which then moves away to an unlocated discussion of
'styles', to attempt to identify two factors: the *internal
organization* of the particular formation; and its *proposed
and actual relations to other organizations* in the same field
and to society more generally.

Internal organization

We have already discussed several examples of internal
organization, and can now provisionally classify them as
follows:

(i) those based on *formal membership*, with varying modes of
internal authority or decision, and of constitution and election;
(ii) those not based on formal membership, but organized
around some *collective public manifestation*, such as an
exhibition, a group press or periodical, or an explicit manifesto;
(iii) those not based on formal membership or any sustained
collective public manifestation, but in which there is *conscious
association or group identification*, either informally or
occasionally manifested, or at times limited to immediate
working or more general relations.

An example of (i), following many earlier kinds of guild,

compagnonnage and brotherhood, is the German *Brother-hood* (later *Order*) of St Luke. An example of (ii) is the English Pre-Raphaelite Brotherhood, with its periodical *The Germ*, or the German *Der Blaue Reiter*, with a book of the same title (by one of its founders, Marc) and a collective exhibition. An example of (iii) is the French *Nabis*, who met regularly but otherwise collaborated only in a private gallery exhibition.

These general classifications, of course with some cases of overlap, take us some way in the analysis of groups based on a single art or on two or three related arts. They are all in this sense working organizations, whether or not they proclaim other more general objectives. Many cultural formations have of course been restricted in this way.

But already in some nineteenth-century cases, and commonly in the twentieth century, a group has formed around some much more general programme, including many or indeed all arts, and often additionally, in relation to this, some very general cultural (and often 'political') position. The best examples are the *Futurists*, from 1909, bringing together painters, sculptors and writers but also proclaiming general (though aesthetically related) positions on the machine, war and danger, and the necessary destruction of the past; the *Surrealists*, from 1922, again bringing together painters and writers, but also relating their work, and justifying it, in terms of general positions on the unconscious, the irrational and dream-activity.

Clearly these are still working groups, usually of type (ii), with a manifesto, a periodical and exhibitions, but there has also been a change of some kind in their social relations, and this can best be understood by the second kind of analysis, of the proposed and actual relations with all those beyond the group.

External relations

We can provisionally classify types of external relations in cultural formations as follows:

(a) *Specializing*, as in the cases of sustaining or promoting work in a particular medium or branch of an art, and in some circumstances a particular style;

(b) *alternative*, as in the cases of the provision of alternative facilities for the production, exhibition or publication of certain kinds of work, where it is believed that existing institutions exclude or tend to exclude these;

(c) *oppositional*, in which the cases represented by (b) are raised to active opposition to the established institutions, or more generally to the conditions within which these exist.

An example of (a) at its simplest is the English *Royal Society of Painter-Etchers and Engravers*, from 1880, or, with some complications, the contemporary English Ruralists. Examples of (b) range from the *New English Art Club* of 1885 to the *Société des Artistes Indépendants* of 1884; such cases are especially numerous. Examples of (c) include the *Futurists*, the *Dadaists* and the *Surrealists*.

There are many complex problems of interpretation, in specific cases, within these general terms. Yet it is of the greatest importance to make such distinctions within what is normally either an unanalysed category – free cultural association – or at best an indiscriminate range.

Thus it is only the *specializing* groups which fit easily into the familiar category of an open or plural society. Such groups can properly be described in terms of free association within a generally accepted cultural diversity, though it must be noted that even here, in many cases, the diversity is established by these initiatives, rather than prepared for them, and that in the cases of particular branches of an art the initiatives often involve significant local conflict.

The genuinely alternative groups go beyond this, since

their critique of the available established institutions, usually in the same general kind of cultural activity, is at least implicit, and is often, as in the typical cases of the secessions, explicit and direct. While the new group can be satisfied by the establishment of alternative facilities, which give it public presence and identity, its distinction from oppositional groups is reasonably clear. Yet it has often happened that attacks on such alternative groups, by established opinion, have shifted them into conscious opposition as distinct from conscious dissent or the offering of a conscious alternative.

However, even in these cases, there is an important difference from the fully oppositional groups, which characteristically begin with attacks on prevailing art forms and cultural institutions, and often with further attacks on the general conditions which are believed to be sustaining them.

There is no obviously regular relation, in this range of formations, between types of internal organization and types of external relation. It is often the case that the specializing groups are of type (i), with formal membership, but they have also been of types (ii) and (iii). Most alternative and oppositional groups have been of type (ii), though there are early cases of type (i) and some later cases of type (iii). But then the problem of the relation between internal and external modes cannot be considered at this formal level only. It has to be reinserted into questions of historical change and of the character of the general social order.

4 Fractions, dissidents and rebels

There appears to be a very marked increase of every kind of independent cultural formation from the middle of the nineteenth century. The proliferation of independent specializing groups can be largely explained in terms of two kinds of development, themselves related: first, the increasing organization and specialization of the market, including its emphasis on the division of labour; second, the growth of a liberal idea of society and its culture, with a corresponding expectation or tolerance of diverse kinds of work. The formation of specialized groups, by trade or by style or tendency, served either to organize and regulate market relations or to bring a body of work to public attention. Often, of course, these were different forms of the same general relations, though the latter cannot be reduced to the former, in all or even a majority of cases.

The alternative and oppositional groups evidently owe something, perhaps much, to the same general conditions. But the (often severe) tensions and conflicts so evident in their formation make it impossible to rest on explanations in market and liberal terms. We have to note, first, an increasing generalization and development of the idea that the practice and values of art are neglected by, or have to be distinguished from, or are superior or hostile to the dominant values of 'modern' society. This range of ideas is complex, and its social history equally so. Its social bases include: (i) the crisis, for many artists, of the transition from patronage to the market; (ii) the crisis, in certain arts, of the transition from handwork to machine production (see Chapter 4, below); (iii) crises within both patronage and the market, in a period of intense and general social conflict; (iv) the attachment of certain groups to a pre-capitalist and/or pre-democratic social order, in which some arts had been accorded privilege within a general privilege; (v) the attachment of other groups to the democratization of the social order, as part of the process of general liberation and human enrichment to which the arts, if they were allowed, could contribute: (vi) a more general opposition, often overlapping and even seeming to unite these diverse political views, to the practices and values of a 'commercial' and 'mechanical' civilization, from which the practice and values of the arts could be distinguished.

The period in which these ideas were becoming general, from the late eighteenth century, is also the period of the attempted distinction between ('external') 'civilization' and ('internal' or 'human') 'culture'. It is moreover the period of the newly general modern meanings of 'the arts' and 'the artist', as terms indicating more than specific practices and practitioners and now centrally including conceptions of general (and then often alternative or oppositional) values.

The independent formations, alternative and oppositional, are directly related to this complex process and set of ideas. Yet the possibility of actually establishing effective independent formations depended, obviously, on general social conditions. This is why, though the ideas were becoming common from the late eighteenth century, effective alternative and oppositional formations became common only in the second half of the nineteenth century and increased markedly towards the end of the century.

One factor in this development, within particular societies, was change in the internal structure of the dominant classes. Within aristocratic and mercantile societies, conflicts about style and tendency, as well as more general social and economic tensions and conflicts in arts practice, were often resolved, or could be attempted to be resolved, by movement from one patron or kind of patron or intermediary to another. This continued, obviously, in early market conditions. But in the new circumstances of established art institutions, fundamentally in relation to an established arts market, the movement towards independent associative formations was inevitable. Recurrent problems of the imposition or privilege of certain styles and tendencies, of methods of selection and of publicity, and then of both general and commercial advantage, might in some cases (usually unsuccessfully) be individually negotiated. But they were much more readily negotiable through association, which was already a basic general tendency in most other social activities. Yet the new for mations were by no means always, and in many cases not at all, defensive. And this in turn depended on the emer gence, within the dominant social order itself, of actual or potential supportive groups. It is at this point, in critical relation to some of the independent groups, that we must introduce the concept of the *class fraction*.

Class fractions

Some examples may clarify this inherently difficult concept. We can look at three important English cultural formations: Godwin and his circle, in the late eighteenth century; the Pre-Raphaelite Brotherhood, in the mid nineteenth century; and the Bloomsbury Group, in the early twentieth century.

We must remember, first, that a social class is by no means always culturally monolithic. In this as in other respects particular groups within a class may be rising or falling in importance, according to the general develop ment of the class and the society. Moreover, groups within a class may have alternative (received or developed) cultural, often religious, affiliations which are not charac teristic of the class as a whole. Again, in any established class, there are processes of internal differentiation, often by types of work. From all these situations, possible alternative bases for variations in cultural production can exist. Additionally, there is a basis for variations in the changing relations between a particular class and other classes.

Godwin and his circle

What is now commonly described, in English cultural history, as 'William Godwin and his Circle', is an especially interesting example, both substantially and as a problem in the analysis of formations. From its familiar title it indicates something like a 'school', centred on the ideas of one writer, and this is not unreasonable, since in the 1790s there were conscious 'Godwinians' and Godwin's best known work, *Political Justice*, was widely and directly influential.

Yet it is soon clear that we have to see Godwin himself within a much wider and more general social formation. This can be directly defined in two ways: first, as the radical wing of English religious dissent, moving towards rationalism; second, as a radical political grouping, concerned with parliamentary reform, the extension of education and the removal of obstacles to free intellectual inquiry. This general formation is widely evident from the 1770s, and is directly connected with the most progressive elements of the industrial bourgeoisie, with their attachments to free enquiry and to a rational science.

Thus, within the bourgeoisie as a whole, we find a particular formation which (a) is rising in importance and (b) has distinct religious and intellectual affiliations. This wide formation then encountered a particular crisis, of internal relations but especially of external relations with other classes and with the dominant social order, in the specific historical situation of responses to the French Revolution. The most enthusiastic defenders of the revolution, and advocates of comparable political changes in England, were to be found mainly here. Yet what had previously been an alternative tendency within the general social order, and in some respects a central tendency within the rising industrial bourgeoisie, was now, in this crisis, shifted into an oppositional tendency. Its explicit political arguments were met not only by counter-arguments but by direct State repression, culminating in 1794. It was within this crisis of the broader social formation that the particular cultural formation of the circle around Godwin became significant.

As a cultural formation it was of type (iii), though there were overlaps to membership of political societies, within the broad formation (e.g., the Revolution Society). But while its range of activities and interests was broad, its cultural identity can best be defined in a particular cultural form, which was in effect a new kind of novel. The intellectual principles which were common to the broad formation – open rational inquiry, the development of morality through education, opposition to oppression and to arbitrary laws – were specifically composed into novels which integrated individual lives and social and moral circumstances by a new formal integration of 'character' and 'plot', with the founding assumption that character and action grew together out of circumstances and could be altered only by their general alteration. Elisabeth Inchbald's *A Simple Story* (1791), Thomas Holcroft's *Anna St Ives* (1792) and Godwin's *Things as They Are* (*Caleb Williams*) (1794) are major examples, and we can associate with these Mary Wollstonecraft's unfinished *The Wrongs of Woman* (1798).

The cultural formation, at this level, is still alternative, but in the crisis of those years it was both necessarily involved in political activities, with direct and dangerous consequences, and in an overlap between what might in a different period be seen as separate kinds of practice; as Godwin justly observed in 1794, 'the humble novelist might be shown to be constructively a traitor'. In fact, this crisis directly entered the form, as a crisis of the principles underlying the formation, in Godwin's two (radically different) endings to *Things as They Are*, of which the latter, written at the time of greatest danger, marks the transition to a new and more subjective form. Thus the alternative formation, forced by prejudice and repression into opposition, became again alternative, by an internal change and adaptation.

Godwin and his circle, after this shift (1794-7), have a quite different cultural importance, with Godwin relatively isolated but with continuing influence on a new formation – that around Shelley, who married the daughter of Godwin and Mary Wollstonecraft. But the authors of *Queen Mab* and of *Frankenstein*, between 1810 and 1820, belong to a distinct and different formation.

The Pre-Raphaelite Brotherhood

The Pre-Raphaelite Brotherhood is at first sight a much simpler kind of formation. Founded by three young painters in 1848, it published a periodical (*The Germ*, 1850) and proclaimed common artistic principles: a rejection of academic conventions, and an attachment to 'attentive observation of inexhaustible nature'. As often happens in such cases, a distinct style was evolved during the early stages of each painter's development, but by the time of their full development they had diverged. Yet, in the most significant period, a set of shared attitudes to painting and to poetry, and through these to more general cultural questions, was distinctly established.

By contrast with Godwin and his circle, who grew out of a broad and rising general formation, at first not in critical relations with its own class, the Pre-Raphaelites, who were in majority from families of the commercial bourgeoisie, were in conscious opposition to the main cultural tendencies of their class, though they may finally be seen as articulating and expressing them. In fact, they found, in majority, commercial bourgeois (usually provincial) patrons, to whom their naturalism was acceptable. But this naturalism was mixed, from the beginning, with an explicit 'medievalism': an attachment to a certain romantic and decorative kind of beauty, which was also – and in the end very explicitly – a critique of the ugliness of nineteenth-century commercial and industrial civilization. At this point, inevitably, they were dissidents from their class, and in one sense rebels against it, but in a specializing way, in that they found in the arts of painting and poetry an *alternative* to the dominant social and cultural order. With this sense of a specialized alternative went a certain set of alternative moral and social attitudes, much more open and relaxed ('bohemian') than the norms of their class.

Although the early work of the Pre-Raphaelites was heavily criticized, by established opinion, they came through, in majority, as the established painters of an immediately succeeding generation. This often though by no means invariably happens with such formations. In this case it was probably a matter of a commercial bourgeoisie, itself still rising in importance, which had not yet found its styles in art. Yet, while this may be generally true, there were other elements in the original position, involving a more thorough opposition to commercial modes and alongside this position attitudes to manual labour, and to the practice of arts and crafts. This can be seen most notably in William Morris, who began under the influence of the group and in much of his practice clearly stayed within their cultural formation, yet who at a later period (the 1880s) developed the dissent from commercial civilization into outright opposition to the whole capitalist order. By the time of that development, however, there was a linkage with other formations, mainly political (socialist) in the quite different social situation of the 1880s, and the specifics of the Pre-Raphaelite formation, though influential, lay far behind.

Bloomsbury

Godwin and his circle had grown out of a relatively broad tendency within the rising industrial bourgeoisie, but was then, as a specific formation, forced into crisis – into a dissidence verging on rebellion – within a general crisis of the social order, itself still politically directed by another class, the ruling landed aristocracy. The Pre-Raphaelites were a specializing formation with ambiguous and eventually alternative relations with a rising commercial bourgeoisie: dissident but at some levels representative of their still forming cultural (decorative) intentions. The later phase, around Morris, belongs to a different phase of the social order, defined primarily by relations with a more organized working class. The cultural formation we know as Bloomsbury is very different from both. It is especially this formation which enables us to define the difficult concept of a fraction.

'Bloomsbury' is clearly a formation of type (iii). Indeed its members often denied that they belonged to any 'group'; they were, they said, primarily friends, with certain family connections, who found some definition (and their group name) from the district of London where a number of them lived. There is no need to deny these elements of their self-description; indeed it is important to recognize that certain cultural formations occur in exactly this way. Yet we do not have to look far into Bloomsbury as an active group to find some of the more fundamental features of an authentic cultural formation.

Thus they were, in majority, from professional and administrative families, and grew up within the newly regularized (reformed) educational system of 'public' school and university. Their leading members (Woolf, Keynes, Strachey) met at Cambridge. The professional and administrative sectors of the now dominant social class (itself a fusion of the high bourgeoisie and the landed aristocracy) had become increasingly important in the new social order of liberal imperialist England; indeed the educational system had been reformed, at its higher levels, primarily for their production. The cultural interests of this general sector, defined by specific kinds of *educational* achievement, can be clearly distinguished from those of the directly industrial and commercial sectors of the same dominant class. Thus they are a fraction of the ruling class in the sense both that they belong integrally to it, directly serving the dominant social order, and that they are a coherent division of it, defined by the values of a specific higher education: the possession of a general, rather than a merely national and class-bound, culture; and the practice of specific intellectual and professional skills. It is significant, and ironic, that their twentieth-century successors were to define them as an 'intellectual *aristocracy*'.

Bloomsbury was a formation within this fraction. It was genuinely dissident, for two reasons. First, it expressed its values in a more absolute form. It insisted on wholly open intellectual inquiry, and on a related entire tolerance. It therefore found itself in opposition to what it regarded as the stupidity, incompetence and prejudice of the actual holders of political and economic power. Second, it was based in and expressed a paradox: that the educational reform had been primarily for men; women were still relatively excluded. The girls of the same families – included in the formation by these direct relationships – shared the same interests but were, in majority, beyond the immediate formative system.

Thus Bloomsbury came to criticize the dominant order over a wide range: for its militarism; for its repressive colonialism; for its unmanaged capitalism; for its sexual inequalities; for its rigidities of manners; for its hypocrisies; for its indifference to the arts. Its view of a more civilized order involved at once the removal of unreasonable restraints and the sensible management of the necessary political and economic framework of life. With these conditions fulfilled, generally or for the time being locally, people would live as free and tolerant individuals, finding their deepest values in the consequent kinds of human diversity and intimacy. Thus the extreme subjectivism of, for example, the novels of Virginia Woolf, belongs within the same formation as the economic interventionism of Keynes, who wanted not only to preserve the economic system by rationalizing it, but to do this so that, within that achieved stability, the real processes of civilized life could be extended, undisturbed.

In the course of their work, which they characteristically, in the terms of their sector, did not see as collective but as a series of *specialist* contributions, they intersected and overlapped with other groupings and other classes. In their critique of unmanaged capitalism and of colonialism this was especially so, and, together with the related Fabians, they had important influence on the evolution of the working-class Labour Party into a specific kind of social democracy. In their real critique of the old order, they were also, often, both isolated and mocked. Yet they remained, practically and culturally, a fractional formation, and this can be seen especially with the advantage of hindsight, since it is now evident that they were expressing at once the highest values of the bourgeois tradition and the necessary next phase of a bourgeois social and cultural order.

Simple and complex formations

We can all see the complexities of any specific analyses of cultural formations. These brief examples are given, in bare outline, to indicate some possible procedures. To the considerations already adduced – modes of internal and of external relations – we can add a distinction, evident between the Pre-Raphaelites on the one hand and both the Godwinians and Bloomsbury on the other, between relatively simple and relatively complex formations, in terms of the area – the actual grouping of practices – which the formation represents.

Thus Bloomsbury, with its combination of writing, painting, philosophy, political theory and economics, is especially complex, at the level of practice, by comparison with the Pre-Raphaelite painters and poets. This affects both their internal and external modes of organization. Characteristically, the internal organization of Bloomsbury, beyond its status as a group of friends and neighbours, and its meetings to read memoirs, was a private but eventually general publishing house (the Hogarth Press) which published over its whole range.

We can see also, as between the Godwinians and Bloomsbury, that the external relations of such formations are not only a matter of internally defined *intentions*, but of the actual and possible relations of the whole social order. Thus, when we see the often remarkable similarity between the principles of the Godwinians and of Bloomsbury, and the external relations implied by these – a rational and tolerant group wishing to extend reason and tolerance, where necessary by radical reform – we find also that we cannot stay on this level, since the actual external relations were also determined *by others*. The Godwinians were not only historically earlier, and therefore more exposed. They were also an advanced element of a rising but not yet dominant class, as distinct from Bloomsbury's status as a fraction of dominance. That the Godwinians were politically repressed was a function of these general class relations, as well of the severity of the historical crisis. At another and crucial level, we find that the Godwinians were only barely able to sustain themselves, financially, in dissent; they depended, in practice, on the general market. In the case of Bloomsbury, changes in the general order, and especially the establishment of a solid sector of professional and intellectual employment, made independent survival much more practicable.

National and 'paranational' formations

The examples given so far relate to developments within a single national social order. Such national formations have continued to be important, but in the twentieth century there has been a marked development of certain kinds of 'international' – or, better, 'paranational' – cultural formation. By the mid-twentieth century this can be clearly related to the institution of an effective world market in some sectors of art, music and literature, and to the corresponding (but not always dependent) sense of larger effective cultures ('European literature', 'Western music', 'Twentieth-century art'). The sociology of such developments is at a different and much broader level than that of cultural formations. Yet the broader developments were in some ways preceded by an important new kind of cultural formation which has to be distinguished from national groups. This can be seen most readily in the development of the concept of the 'avant garde'.

No full social analysis of avant-garde movements has yet, to my knowledge, been undertaken, and many of the relevant facts have still to be empirically established. But, looking broadly at various avant-garde movements between the 1890s and the 1920s, we can propose certain hypotheses which can be tested by research. First, that the avant-garde movements have, typically, a metropolitan base (where 'metropolitan' must be distinguished from both 'urban' and 'national capital' definitions, its key factors being a relative [especially cultural] autonomy and a degree of internationalization, itself often related to imperialism). Second, that a high proportion of the contributors to avant-garde movements were immigrants to such a metropolis, not only from outlying national regions but from other and smaller national cultures, now often seen as culturally provincial in relation to the metropolis (e.g., the typical figure of Guillaume Apollinaire – born Wilhelm Apollinaris de Kostrowitzki – and his eventual role in Paris). Third, that certain factors in avant-garde culture, and especially the conscious breaks from 'traditional' styles, have to be analysed not only in formal terms but within the sociology of metropolitan encounters and associations between immigrants who share no common language but that of the metropolis and whose other (including visual) received sign-systems have become distanced or irrelevant. This would be a traceable social factor within the often noted innovations in attitudes to language and to the received visual significance of objects. Fourth, that such avant-garde formations, developing specific and distanced styles within the metropolis, at once reflect and compose kinds of consciousness and practice which become increasingly relevant to a social order itself developing in the directions of metropolitan and international significance beyond the nation-state and its provinces, and of a correspondingly high cultural mobility (cf. the relations between the Paris of 1890–1930 and the New York of 1940–70). Fifth, that the internal social conditions of a metropolis, combining at once the metropolitan concentration of wealth and the internal pluralism of its metropolitan-immigrant functions, create especially favourable supportive conditions for dissident groups.

It is not yet known whether research would confirm

these hypotheses of the character of certain distinct twentieth-century paranational cultural formations, though they provide an initial basis for considering the contradictory character of the history of the avant-garde movements: that they represent sharp and even violent breaks with received and traditional practices (a dissidence or revolt rather than a literal avant garde); and yet that they become (in ways separable from the important facts of their dilution and commercial exploitation) the dominant culture of a succeeding metropolitan and paranational period.

Formations, history and individuals

These brief examples should show at once the possibilities and the limits of formational analysis. The limits are especially clear. No full account of a particular formation or kind of formation can be given without extending description and analysis into general history, where the whole social order and all its classes and formations can be taken properly into account. All that formational analysis can do is to put sociological questions to that general history and, at times, from these questions, suggest new areas for detailed research.

Again, no full account of a formation can be given without attending to individual differences inside it. Formations of the more modern kinds may be seen to occur, typically, at points of transition and intersection within a complex social history, but the individuals who at once compose the formations and are composed by them have a further complex range of diverse positions, interests and influences, some of which are resolved (if at times only temporarily) by the formations, others of which remain as internal differences, as tensions, and often as the grounds for subsequent divergences, breakaways, breakups and further attempted formations.

Thus no sociological analysis of formations can replace either general history or these more specific individual studies. Yet it is still an indispensable kind of analysis, since there is normally a very wide gap between, on the one hand, general history and the associated general history of particular arts, and, on the other hand, individual studies. It is, then, by learning to analyse the nature and the diversity of cultural formations – in close association, as is later argued, with the analysis of cultural forms – that we can move towards a more adequate understanding of the direct social processes of cultural production.

4 Means of Production

We have been analysing social institutions and formations in cultural production, in their variably manifest forms. Yet it is clear that there is another kind of social history of cultural production, in its most general sense, and that this is central to its sociology.

The invention and development of the material means of cultural production is a remarkable chapter of human history, yet it is usually underplayed, by comparison with the invention and development of what are more easily seen as forms of material production, in food, tools, shelter and utilities. Indeed a common ideological position marks this latter area off as 'material', by contrast with the 'cultural' or, in the more common emphases, the 'artistic' or the 'spiritual'.

Yet we do not have unreasonably to assimilate cultural practice to this area of the satisfaction of basic human needs to realize that, whatever purposes cultural practice may serve, its means of production are unarguably material. Indeed, instead of starting from the misleading contrast between 'material' and 'cultural', we have to define two areas for analysis: first, the relations between these material means and the social forms within which they are used (this is of course a general problem in social analysis, but the discussion is limited, here, to cultural means and forms); and, second, the relations between these material means and social forms and the specific (artistic) forms which are a manifest cultural production (these will be discussed in the succeeding chapters).

We can make, first, an important general distinction, with continuing social and sociological effects, between (i) that class of material means which depends wholly or mainly on inherent, constituted physical resources, and (ii) that other class which depends wholly or mainly on the use or transformation of non-human material objects and forces. No history of the arts can be written without full attention to both. The arts of spoken poetry, of song and of dance are obvious examples of the former, as are painting and sculpture of the latter. And then what is interesting is that whatever their exact priority (which may perhaps never be determined) each of these kinds is very early indeed in human culture. Moreover each kind has continued to be important; it is not a simple question of successive stages.

It is often said, persuasively, that men entered into social relations in the course of using or transforming the non-human material world. But this should never carry the implication (common in some branches of theory) that no social relations were entered into in the course of using and developing inherent and constituted physical resources. Both forms of development are already evident at an evolutionary stage, and there, as in later more consciously social development, the analytically separable processes are usually in practice inextricable. Yet because social relations, and especially changes in social relations, are often more evident in cases of developments in the use or transformation of non-human material objects and forces, it is worth emphasizing the manifest social character of the other kind of development.

Development of inherent resources

The achievement of language, in any full sense, lies within the complex transition from the evolutionary to the social. The development of species-inherited 'non-verbal communication' (postures, gestures, facial expressions) into cultural forms and variations of these basic possibilities is within the same complex transition. But even if the 'social' stage is moved forward (tendentiously) to the point at which these developed resources can be said to 'already' exist, it is impossible to overlook the extraordinary social history of the institution of systems for their further cultural development.

Dance, song and speech

There is, for example, the amazing social development of all the forms of dance, over a range from complex traditional forms to prolonged professional training. There is the same remarkable development in ways of using the human voice in singing and in certain specifically formal kinds of speech. We can observe a familiar transition from a relatively general training, in these highly valued skills, to degrees of specialization and professionalization in more complex societies, but some forms of specialization seem to be remarkably early and, on the other hand, there are probably no societies in which relatively general training in forms of these basic skills is not attempted.

This relative generality of development is of great sociological importance, by contrast with the much more uneven and often specialized and exclusive development of forms of cultural production which depend on the use or transformation of non-human resources. In complex societies there is a significant and often decisive unevenness, as the systems which train these inherent and constituted resources become more professional and more masterly. But (the more so while elements of the most general training persist) certain crucial human and social connections, or potential connections, are still there, in the shared resources of which these are developments. It is then not at all surprising that dancing and singing, in their most general forms, have been and have remained, in complex as in in simple societies, the most widespread and popular cultural practices.

Uses of non-human means

It is when we turn to practices based (in whole or in part) on the use or transformation of non-human material objects and forces that the social relations become much more complex and variable. We can begin with a preliminary distinction of types of such practice, as follows:

(i) *combination* of the use of external objects with the use of inherent physical resources, over a range from the use of paint, masks and costume in dance to the use of masks, costume and scenery in acted drama;

(ii) *development of instruments* of new kinds of performance, as notably in musical instruments;

(iii) selection, transformation and production of *separable objects*, which then carry cultural significance, as in the use of clay, metal, stone and pigment in sculpture and painting;

(iv) development of *separable material systems of signification*, devised for cultural significance, as most notably in writing;

(v) development of *complex amplificatory, extending and reproductive technical systems*, which make possible new kinds of presentation of all the preceding types, but also new kinds of presentation of practices still otherwise based on the use of inherent and constituted resources.

In the matter of social relations, the first three types are relatively continuous with those based on inherent resources, while the fourth and fifth types introduce problems of relationship of quite new kinds.

Problems of access

There is usually some generality of access to at least some of the techniques involved in the first three types. Where this is so, the relation between some form of general training and highly developed specialist training is not necessarily more difficult than in the comparable relation in the training of inherent physical resources. On the other hand, as a culture becomes richer and more complex, involving many more artistic techniques developed to a high degree of specialization, the social distance of many practices becomes much greater, and there is a virtually inevitable if always complex set of divisions between participants and spectators in the various arts. These important divisions affect the character of modern cultures, to the point where the social relations between artists and ('their') spectators or 'publics' can seem the only kind that needs to be considered.

Yet, first, that outcome of specialization which is an assumed general division between those who create and perform and those who merely receive is not significantly greater at this level of material techniques than at the level of systems of training of inherent resources. Indeed, second, while there are connections between at least some elementary general training and the advanced forms of professional training, and while access to these advanced forms, for those who want it, is still relatively open, the form of division between 'artist' and 'public' need not be at all of a damaging kind; it is often in practice a willing and serious interchange between professionals and those interested in the highest development of these skills. The very different case of a generalized division, between

'creators' and 'spectators', may in part be influenced by
such relations, but is not fully generated or confirmed
there. Indeed it is only, or at least primarily, in the
development of material techniques of the fourth and fifth
types that what is at first not much more than a relatively
open specialization and diversity of attention becomes a
formative and even determining set of *divisive* social
relations.

There are a number of reasons why this is so. For some
centuries the first reason seemed simple, though it has been
greatly complicated by the most recent technical developments. If you are watching some highly developed dance
form, or some elaborately staged drama, or listening to
highly developed music, or looking at highly developed
sculpture or painting, you have at least some given mode of
access to each art. You can at least see or hear, which has
been part of your ordinary physical development. And
then, though in varying degrees, you can see or hear these
specific kinds of work: relatively easily if they are specific
forms of your own culture; with more difficulty, and
sometimes with absolute difficulty, if they are forms of
some other, especially remote culture, or if your own
culture is deeply divided and these forms come from an
area that is strange to you.

Through all these varying degrees of access, there is still,
in work in these techniques, some connection of inherent
resources. It has been possible for many of us, for example,
to respond to dance from quite other cultures, and to
sculpture, carving and painting not only from other
cultures but from other, often very remote, times. The
connection of inherent resources, often deepened by what
may be shared rhythmic and perceptual qualities in our
species, offers at least some degree of relatively unmediated
access. The cultural specialization which is also present,
with varying degrees of difficulty, in these especially

physical forms is usually more of a problem in at least some music, where there have been some very radical divergences in systems and in instruments. But again, over a surprisingly wide area, and especially in song and in the simpler instruments, some degree of relatively unmediated access is available, with some shared rhythmic resources, possibly of the whole species, as an important factor. Drama, inevitably, is more culturally specialized by language, but in many of its other elements of movement and scene it is widely and inherently accessible, as is clear in mime and was very evident in the silent film.

Writing

The point of these examples is not to underestimate the difficulties of social relations and cultural access in these types of cultural technique, but to show, by contrast, the qualitative difference when we come to such material systems as writing. For though writing shares, at a later stage, all the difficulties mentioned – of degrees of familiarity with specific forms, and of the effects of cultural specialization, as most notably in language – it has also, from the beginning, a radically different status, as a technique. Thus while anyone in the world, with normal physical resources, can watch dance or look at sculpture or listen to music, still some forty per cent of the world's present inhabitants can make no contact whatever with a piece of writing, and in earlier periods this percentage was very much larger. Writing as a cultural technique is wholly dependent on forms of specialized training, not only (as became common in other techniques) for producers but also, and crucially, for receivers. Instead of being a development of an inherent or generally available faculty, it is a specialized technique wholly dependent on specific training. It is then not surprising that for a very long period the most difficult problems in the social relations of cultural practice revolved around the question of literacy.

Social relations of writing

The earliest forms of writing were developed by and confined to very limited specialist (usually official) groups; they were later somewhat extended in continued urban development and in merchant trade. The general cultural problem was not at this stage acute, for writing was still primarily a technique of administration, record and contract. It was in the next stage, when writing came to carry an increasing proportion of law, learning, religion and history, previously carried in oral forms, that very marked cultural divisions, already socially present in pre-literate societies, became, as it were, technically stabilized.

In the further powerful development of all these uses, and even when some other social relations were changing, this form of stratification of access became more and more important. Increasingly, also, the oral 'literature' of pre-literate or marginally literate societies was, through many complex stages, transferred to this new material technique, and further developed through it. Writing moved from (i) a supporting and recording function, in societies in which oral composition and tradition were still predominant, through (ii) a stage in which this function was joined by written composition for oral performance and (iii) a further stage in which composition was additionally written only to be read, to (iv) that later and very familiar stage in which most or virtually all composition was written to be silently read, and was at last, for this reason, generalized as 'literature'.

The great advantages of writing, with its enormous expansion of newly possible kinds of continuity and access, have been counterpointed, throughout, by the radical disadvantages of its inherent specialization of the faculty of reception. It is only in the last hundred and fifty years, in any culture, that a majority of people have had even minimal access to this technique which already, over two millennia, had been carrying a major part of human culture. The consequences of this long (and in many places continuing) cultural division have been very great, and the confusion of developments beyond it, in societies at last becoming generally literate, is still very much with us.

Amplification, extension and reproduction

But at this point, decisively, techniques of the new fifth type become relevant and even determining. There are always internal constraints on any kind of notational or visual-symbolic signifying system, since these depend on an absolutely or relatively complete possession of the relevant (social as technical) systematic information. But while the objects embodying these systems are themselves relatively fixed and single, there is a correspondence (usually of a caste kind) between the internal systematic constraints and internal (often hierarchical) social relations.

Reproduction of images

The new techniques of deliberate reproduction and circulation are then of great sociological significance. In their earliest examples, as seals, coins and medals, they were directly connected with extending trade and with extending political empire. The reproducible symbolic visual image became a mode of defining a social area of credit or of power. In the case of political empire, the decisive production and reproduction of an area of power was of course by other (military and political) means, though at the level of reproduction use of the reproducible image of authority became and has remained very important. In the case of extended trade, the reproducible image as currency (often stamped on material of intrinsic value) became quite decisive in the reproduction of trading relationships, and was also a leading factor in the production of new kinds of trade. In either case the reproducible image was still primarily a function of political or economic relationships.

It was in the field of cult and religious objects, of decorative and decorated-utilitarian articles, and of what can eventually be distinguished as, in a modern sense, works of art, that reproductive technology became a major cultural mode. The leading technique was that of casting, and we can find it, from early times, across a very wide range. It was a major factor in the extension of cults and religions, from the votive statuette to the image of a god. It was also very evident in political-cultural uses, as in the portrait-busts of kings and emperors. Many, perhaps most, of these objects are seen now as 'works of art', in one sense justly, because of their fine workmanship, but in another sense misleadingly, since their primary function, especially in this area of reproduction and deliberate circulation, was evidently religious or ideological. What can properly be called art is still, in majority, an inherent and inseparable element of some other purpose.

Graphic reproduction

This remains true in the next decisive technical stage, that of graphic reproduction. In fourth-century-BC Athens it was possible to buy manuscripts reproduced by hand-copying at relatively low cost, and the *scriptoria* in which such copying was done – there is a reference in Pliny the Younger to an edition of a thousand copies – remained important through Roman to medieval times. But techniques of reproducing graphic images – illustrations – were very slow to develop. The woodcut reproducible illustration, and even wooden letters for printing, made their first appearance in China, but it was as late as the fourteenth century in Europe before paper (brought to Europe by the Arabs in the late twelfth century, when the traditional material of parchment was in short supply) began to be extensively used for the new technology of xylography: repeatable woodcut designs in fabrics extended to rapidly reproducible illustrations. There was then a huge trade in religious and moral pictures of this reproduced kind, often in series and printed literally by the million. Then, in the fifteenth century, the casting of metal type was combined with developments in kinds of press and of ink to make the printing of texts possible, and the full range of rapid and accurate graphic reproduction was at last available.

Social effects of reproduction systems

The social effects of this complex of technical changes have been diverse. On the one hand it is clear that the techniques of physical reproduction were still largely employed within the modes of general social and cultural reproduction. This is especially evident in the huge production of prints of Christ and the saints, and in the extensive printing of bibles, psalters and indulgences. But then there are also, in printing, overlapping cases such as calendars, almanacs and grammars, and soon, decisively, the printing and circulation of a whole body of classical literary texts, of other (introduced and reintroduced) forms of thought and learning, and then, finally, of newly produced texts.

It is then clear that, at the very lowest, social and cultural reproduction, in these technologies, is significantly more diverse than in the pre-reproduction phase. This radically affected the position of the writer, the scholar and the artist as producers. The changes correspond, in fact, to the stages of overlap and eventually transition between patronal and market relations. What had been technically and socially achieved was not only extended distribution but that inherent mobility of cultural objects which is crucial to regular market relations. It is interesting that it was in the same period as that of the large-scale production of holy prints on paper that the (moveable) canvas began to replace the wall-fresco as the most common base material for painting.

With this diversity, extended distribution and mobility, came new forms and opportunities of artistic and cultural independence; or, to put it more strictly, forms of direct dependence, within relatively monopolistic social and cultural reproduction, were modified and sometimes replaced by forms of more variable dependence on more diverse modes of such reproduction, and within this diversity there was some significant innovation.

Relations between social and cultural production and reproduction

The most important theoretical indication, from this series and complex of changes, is that of the *variable degrees of symmetry* between cultural production and general social and cultural reproduction. For all practical purposes we can designate such relations in the earliest productive modes as wholly symmetrical. There is an effectively full parity between the purposes of cultural production and this more general social and cultural reproduction. But in some of the early stages of the technical reproduction of cultural production, as most notably in the political empires and the related imposition of religious systems, elements of asymmetry begin to appear, in the relations between dominant and subordinated cultures. In the massively reproductive social orders of the feudal and medieval periods these elements are still evident, and can at times be clearly perceived as asymmetries of a class kind.

Asymmetries

But it is in the new period of widely available physical reproduction of cultural artefacts, within already diversifying social relations, that asymmetries of a more complex kind than those of domination and subordination begin to appear. Many of the leading relations are still of course quite symmetrical, as in the case of the production of religious prints and texts. Indeed in some respects the new technologies of standardized and widely distributed reproduction made certain forms of social and cultural reproduction very much more effective, over a wider range, and in modes distinguishable from direct domination and subordination. But in printing especially – in literature and learning but also in scientific texts, in which accurately reproducible illustration played a crucial part – there was soon an evident asymmetry between the received and relatively rigid forms of social and cultural reproduction and this newly diverse and mobile cultural production and distribution. Many of the most important problems of the social relations of culture take their origin from the appearance of this effective if always variable asymmetry.

Three types of asymmetry

This general condition of asymmetry can be examined in three major areas of tension, conflict and struggle, within which the fact of asymmetry is always a major element. These areas are (i) the organization of licensing, censorship and other similar forms of control, and the struggle against these; (ii) the organization of the market, both in its aspect as a trading area whose purposes, in expansion and profit, may often be in conflict with otherwise dominant political and cultural authorities, and its aspect as a mechanism for commodities in this especially sensitive field, where inherent calculations of profit and scale may impose tensions with other conceptions of art and, at a different level, impose its own new forms of commercial controls; and (iii) the uneven and changing relations between a received and always to some extent recuperated 'popular' (largely oral) culture and the new forms of standardized and increasingly centralized production and reproduction.

(i) Controls and their limits

The struggle for freedom of expression, and the invention of means to control it, are of course both very old. The difficult and often contradictory principles of this age-long argument were memorably expressed as early as Plato's version of the *Apology* of Socrates and, with a different bearing, in his *Republic*. There is also an instructive history in the condemnation and prohibition of books by the medieval church. But changes in the means of production, and especially printing, led to new forms of control, with more emphasis on prevention than on retribution: a direct reflection of the new conditions of rapid and extensive reproduction. In the Church, by a papal bull of 1487, pre-censorship was prescribed, and from 1559 the Index. In England, from 1531, a pre-censorship licensing system was established under secular authority; forms of this system lasted till 1695. The struggle against such controls was long and hard, and it was not, for example, until the mid twentieth century in England, where the struggle had been early and relatively successful, that the last general form of this kind was abolished, in the theatre.

(ii) State and market

But the crucial factor of asymmetry, which had been present throughout in the factors of cheap and rapid (often secret) reproduction and mobility, became more and more evident in the fuller development of the market. Crucial battles were fought over the newspaper, with a new armoury of legal and (very significantly) fiscal (stamp-duty) controls, but both the buoyancy of the market and the growth of liberal opinion eventually prevailed. In its later stages, the conflict settled around two issues: (a) official information, which in modern conditions was of direct political interest to the State; and (b) obscenity, which characteristically only became a major object of legislation in the nineteenth century, with the development of an effective popular market.

Through all these phases, though of course in different ways, we can see the complex asymmetry between the older established institutions of cultural and social reproduction (Church and State) and the new institutions and forces both of the market and of professional and cultural independence. If the conflicts have been most evident in direct cultural production, they have been most complex and most general in the crucial formative area of education, where the direct controls of established institutions of reproduction have been easier to maintain, largely because the influence of market forces has been very much less relevant, and the only major factor of asymmetry has been the (always practically weaker) claim of professional and cultural independence.

Asymmetry between the market and the official reproductive institutions changed in character as the market moved towards universality, especially in the newest means of production and reproduction, above all cinema and television. It is common today to hear complaints from established institutions, which still claim some dominance (now more usually called 'responsibility') in general social and cultural reproduction, against the character of market-dominant cultural production, usually specified as 'sex-and-violence'.

There is, here, a theoretical curiosity. Simple Marxist versions of social and cultural reproduction often elide the bourgeois market with the 'ideological apparatus' of the bourgeois state. Yet it is clear that there is significant and sustained conflict, over some crucial cultural issues, between the state in its simplest form (as in legislation on obscenity or on official information) or the 'apparatus' in its more complex form (as in religious or educational campaigns against 'sex-and-violence' or 'materialism'), and the actual profitable operations of the capitalist market. Such conflicts are evidence of the most significant modern form of asymmetry.

Social relations of asymmetry

This is even clearer when we examine the basic social relations underlying this asymmetry. It is impossible, for example, to take at face value the implied relations between the state, the established cultural institutions, and the market. For the cultural production which is complained of comes in majority from central market institutions which in all other respects (and even, practically, in this one) the state exists to promote and protect, and even, in some cases, from institutions which it directly licenses. This complexity must not be reduced to simple hypocrisy, although there is of course some of that. The basic complexity is one of asymmetry, which in these conditions shows itself as a deepseated contradiction between the reproduction of market relations (both directly, within the market, and indirectly, within state and educational functions) and the consequences of such reproduction in certain sensitive and perhaps crucial areas of public morality, respect for authority and actual crime.

In the last twenty years, in new and decisively extended areas of physical reproduction (notably television and the disc and cassette in popular music), this deepseated contradiction has been especially acute. The interacting factors of (i) a newly effective market among the young, of (ii) some culturally effective initiatives by the young, of which many were quickly taken up by the market, of (iii) a more general unwillingness by the market, in conditions of high competition, to observe the limits and pressures of established cultural reproduction, and yet (iv) the alarm of state and other established institutions at the sources and consequences of such cultural production, have combined to produce a situation of quite remarkable asymmetry. A Marxist book, an anarchist's guide, attacks on the institution of the family, songs celebrating illegal drugs, films and television plays celebrating physical violence or showing crime as justifiable or successful, can and do become, whatever their varying cultural sources, profitable commodities in a market within a state and culture which officially (and no doubt, within the terms of its insoluble contradiction, really) disapproves of or opposes all these things. The older though continuing tensions between cultural authority and cultural independence have been transformed by the increasingly dominant social relations of the new means of production and reproduction.

Market freedoms and controls. In many of these phases, and still in some today, the market has played an objectively liberating role, against the older centralized forms of cultural dominance. This role is still stressed, in many cases justly, by the spokesmen of market relations. Yet to see only this is to simplify the history to the point of misrepresentation. For within market relations two new kinds of control, amounting in some cases to dominance, have become apparent.

First there is the fact that when the work has become a commodity, produced to be sold at a profit, the internal calculations of any such market production lead directly to new forms of cultural control and especially cultural selection. We have become so habituated to market relations that it can seem merely banal to observe that types of work which make a loss will, within market production, be reduced or discontinued, while types which make a profit will be expanded. These effects can be interpreted as the effects of people's choices, and indeed this is often so. But the real process is more complicated, since profitable production is not only a matter of how many people will buy but also – and in some arts crucially – a matter of the real costs of production, properly carried out. Thus, in addition to the general process in which the market registers people's choices and these feed back into selected or discontinued types of production, there is an evident pressure, *at or before* the point of production, to reduce costs: either by improving the technical means of reproduction, or by altering the nature of the work or pressing it into other forms.

It is here, second, that manifest commercial modes of control and selection become, in effect, cultural modes. This is especially clear in the later stages of the market, when the relatively simple relations of speculative production have been joined and in many areas replaced by planned marketing operations in which certain types of work are positively promoted, of course with the corollary that other types are left at best to make their own way. This effect has been most noticeable, for obvious reasons, in the most highly capitalized forms of production. It is the real history of the modern popular newspaper, of the commercial cinema, of the record industry, of art reproduction and, increasingly, of the paperback book. Items within each of these are pre-selected for massive reproduction, and though this may often still fail the general effect is of a relatively formed market, within which the buyer's choice – the original rationale of the market – has been displaced to operate, in majority, within an already selected range.

This works in different degrees in different media. The cinema and the popular newspaper are the most extreme contemporary examples. But a degree of alteration of social relations is evident everywhere. In sophisticated market planning, a certain type of work can be selected at so early a stage, on the basis of a few examples or of some calculated or projected demand, that production, from that stage, no longer originates with the primary producer but is commissioned from him. This can result in a relatively rapid turnover of cultural fashions, as one project of this kind succeeds another, and this area of relatively rapid innovation – often of a minor kind – has been important in the later twentieth century, as a direct function of the expansion and increased rate of internal circulation of the market itself. The difference of such innovation from the more normal processes of cultural and artistic innovation is – always in degree, often in kind – a matter of origins. At its most typical, this new form of innovation is at least primarily a *marketing function*, and this contrasts sharply with other kinds of innovation, which, governed by internal cultural purposes, often find themselves at the very margin of the market or indeed outside it altogether.

On the other hand, the contrast between market-originated and producer-originated work cannot be made absolute, once market conditions have been generalized. For producers often *internalize* known or possible market relationships, and this is a very complex process indeed, ranging from obvious production for the market which is still the work the producer 'always wanted to do', through all the possible compromises between the market demand and the producer's intention, to those cases in which the practical determinations of the market are acknowledged but the original work is still substantially done.

Moreover, the movements of the market can never be separated from more general movements of social and cultural relations. The entry of new social classes, new age-groups and new minorities into the effective cultural market is commonly the result of much more general social change, to which the market has to adapt. The interaction of these more general changes with the complex processes of internal cultural production leads, clearly, to many diverse results. Yet these, finally, have to be set down as *complications* of the market process, and not as factors which override it.

To take any form of cultural production out of the market, by new patronal or public funding, is a very deliberate decision, with its own, sometimes isolating and conserving, effects. Typically, moreover, it is marginal, however important and substantial the arts involved (as now poetry, opera, ballet, and an increasing proportion of orchestral music and of theatre). A new principle of selection, between 'subsidized' and 'commercial', has effects of asymmetry well beyond the simple economic differences. The case for subsidy, to override or protect from the market, is characteristically made in terms of the received arts and their received forms. Innovation, as so often in the market itself, is seen primarily within these received terms.

For of course, though the market is always sensitive to innovations, and must in part of its production promote them, the great bulk of market production is solidly based on known forms and minor variants of known forms. Often seen as restless and innovative, because of its evident novelties, the market is still, by its nature, profoundly reproductive both of known demand ('public taste' as already crystallized) and of known priorities (usually the compatibility of work with the technical, economic and ultimately social means and determinants of its types of production). At the deepest level this is its symmetry with the social order within which it operates, and the 'non-market' or 'subsidized' type of production is often an aspect of this symmetry in that by selecting certain kinds of work for partial exemption from the market – kinds valued within the distribution of preferences within a received social order and a dominant social class – it in one sense protects the market from other kinds of social and cultural challenge.

Yet this relation, marked by many forms of co-operation, interaction and two-way movement between the 'market' and 'subsidized' areas, is nevertheless always precarious, for there can be little real doubt that it is the dominant area, the market, which either determines, or emphasizes and de-emphasizes, prevailing types of production, and there are then the familiar asymmetries: (i) between the notion of a necessary 'high culture' and the pressures of the market on its continued viability; and (ii) between the notion of plural ('liberal') culture and the actual profit-governed market selection of what can be readily distributed or even, in some areas, offered at all. These asymmetries are continually negotiated and re-negotiated, but it is significant that they seem to have settled down, in our own period, mainly along a line of division between newer and older means of production, with the market dominant in the new reproductive technologies and subsidy most evident in the older 'live' forms. And this outcome is not surprising, since the historical connections between the new reproductive technologies and the cultural dominance of market relations is particularly clear.

(iii) Reproduced and popular culture

We have then to look at a third area of asymmetry, directly connected with qualitative changes in the means of cultural production. What is usually said about the invention of printing is that it greatly expanded an earlier minority culture, and at last made it into a majority culture. Yet it is here that we have to distinguish most clearly between a technical invention and a technology, and then further between a technology and its actual or possible social relations.

Already, with the invention of writing, there is a basic asymmetry between use of this powerful new means and ordinary membership of a society. This becomes more marked as the importance of writing increases but the ability to read rises much more slowly. Relations between a still predominantly oral culture and this important and growing sector 'within' it are then especially complex, and the point is soon reached when there is a qualitative difference between the oral area, which all share but to which most are confined, and the literate area, which is of increasing cultural importance but is at once minor and dominant.

Techniques and technologies. The point at which this crucial relation is reached is very variable, in different societies, but we are reminded, everywhere, of the decisive distinctions between a technical invention, a technology and the social relations within which technologies can alone operate. Thus the technology of writing is not only the series of inventions – a script, an alphabet, and materials for its production – which initiate the process, but the mode of distribution of the work thus produced. And this mode of distribution is itself not only technical – manuscript copying and then printing – but depends on a wider technology, primarily determined by social relations, in which the ability to read, which is the true substance of distribution, is itself produced. The invention of printing, a key technical stage in the technology of distribution, had remarkable early effects in that it made technical distribution much easier but in conditions of relatively unaltered social distribution. Moreover, in decisively increasing the importance of the literate culture, it had the effect of a new kind of stratification, in which the cultural but also the social importance of the still oral majority culture declined.

Much of the subsequent development of literacy, and the eventually general extension of printed matter, can then only in one sense be treated as an 'expansion'. Quantitatively it is indeed so, but the cultural specialization of literacy, and then of the true potential of the invention and the technology, led to significant internal hierarchies. The most serious cultural creation and the most authoritative social knowledge were 'in print'. Access to literacy was determined and directed by institutions formed on these assumptions. 'Correctness', even in the matter of speaking a native language, was similarly determined. Relative social position and relative command of this skill became regularly associated. Thus the qualitative nature of the expansion was to an important extent controlled and was never a merely neutral extension.

The internal hierarchies of the print system were of course broadly coherent with more general social hierarchies, or they could not have been so effective. The standardizing, regularizing, authoritative properties often assigned to print as a medium (though many of them are inherent in any writing system) could have full social effect only if they had this broad coherence with general developments in the social and labour processes, to which, however, print was not a mere ancillary, for it was one of the forms of such development. The industrial revolution, among other things, necessarily *produced* general literacy.

Passages from the oral. But what is then especially interesting is that the cultural process of including and incorporating areas of the oral culture into printed forms is very complex indeed, and in some important respects contradictory. There is plenty of evidence of selection and dilution, and indeed struggles over certain socially sensitive passages from speech to print have continued into our own time. There is also much evidence of various ideological representations and transformations of earlier oral social forms, as in songs, ballads, tales and confessions. But the potentials of the technology were never wholly controllable. There was no way to teach a man to read the Bible – a predominant intention in much early education in literacy – which did not also enable him to read the radical press. And this press was there to be read because under a range of pressures from open repression to financial disadvantage some men took initiatives to use the technology for their own as opposed to the dominant social purposes. In many ways, as the technology and its altering social relations became more general, new forms and new areas of experience made their own way into print. The older coherence of a specialized literate culture was challenged alike by these genuine initiatives and by the eventually widespread reproduction of imputed popular material, in speculative and profitable works designed for an expansion seen not as a changing culture but as a new and decisive market.

Changed access to new media. Yet, however extended, the basic process of writing and printing retained at least some elements of mediation. It is, after all, an inherently *notational* rather then a direct system. This is where the next phase of development in the means of cultural production is so significant. For, if in variable ways, the new technologies of cinema, sound broadcasting, sound discs and cassettes, television, video cassettes and tape recorders all embody systems of access which are direct at least in the sense that they are culturally available within normal social development, without any form of selective cultural training.

Of course this does not mean that the technologies are not embedded in specific economic, institutional and cultural systems, or that they do not constitute specific signifying systems, with their own internal forms. But in the matter of the relations between a general oral and a privileged literate culture, the shift is crucial. Within systems quite as impersonal and even more technically complex than the printed book, the manifest cultural relations have this apparent and often real immediacy. Speech modes, however qualified, and indeed the fully colloquial, become public norms in ways that contrast sharply with the period of printed public norms. The tape-recording of this or that speaker is significantly different from a written or printed report of what he said. In the media which are also visual, a range of resources – physical appearance and the effective means of non-verbal communication – is at least added to the written or recorded form, and the effect is often more than addition; it is a change of dimension which appears to restore *presence*, which for the alternative advantages of record and durability writing systems had moved away from.

It is true that, much more than they acknowledge, the new systems derive forms and materials from the accumulation of written material, and from some of the specific hierarchies of print, which are still normally coherent with the social order of the new systems as institutions. Yet, even when this has been allowed for, the balance of forces between the continuing general oral culture and the selective technically transmitted culture has been in at least some respects altered, and with it the nature of the asymmetry between the institutions of cultural production and the broader institutions of general social and cultural reproduction. To explore this more thoroughly we must look at the changes in the social relations of cultural production which came with these new technologies.

New forms of cultural production

From the epoch of a privileged literate culture we have derived a stereotype of the cultural producer as an individual; characteristically an *author*. The root association of this word with the sense of authority is not accidental; the conception of an 'author' is of an autonomous source. We may know that authors work within determinate social and cultural conditions, but we still emphasize the fact of *individual* production. And though we know also that in early periods, and especially and persistently in certain forms – drama, dance, choral song – production was not even in this manifest sense individual but was necessarily of a group kind, still the emphasis on 'the producer', 'the author', remains predominant, because it corresponds quite directly to the manifest conditions of production in writing and in print, and to certain oral forms which directly preceded them. The writer, and then the printer, the sculptor, the composer, are manifestly in that set of specific relations, linked directly with the nature of their immediate means of production.

Group production

In those forms which have always depended on group production, there is not only a contrast with these basically individual uses of the immediate means of production, but, just as crucially, a range of developing relationships, many directly related to changes in the means of production, which amount, finally, to a further qualitative distinction. These changes, at their most general, are, first, the substantial development of the division of labour, inside cultural processes, and, second, forms of class division, related both to the specialized divisions of the process and to the ownership and management of the developed means of production.

We know too little about the internal social relations of some of the earliest collective and collaborative forms to speak with any certainty of that stage. But in general it can be said that authority and direction within cultural production either derived directly from the integral social organization within which such duties were assigned, or, as in the case of classical Greek drama, were assigned within a civic organization and became, in effect, a process of tender and hire. Division of labour, at this stage, is primarily professional; there are actors, singers, musicians, dancers, writers. The problem of co-ordination of these various professional skills was solved in various ways, of which we know very little just because, it seems, no general and abstract solution was stabilized. Even as late as the Elizabethan theatre, where we find an owner or lessee in contractual or hiring relations with a company or with individuals, the processes of internal control of the production are obscure. There is no stabilized figure corresponding to the later producer or director, who does not really appear in theatre until the late nineteenth century. He had been significantly preceded, however, by the actor-manager: a familiar kind of solution, in which a leading member of one of the professional groups – that group which is or seems dominant in the specific process – not only co-ordinates but controls. There had been earlier instances of co-ordination or control by the dramatist or by the composer. But also, either substituting for this, or modifying it, there are many cases of practical internal co-ordination by the *professional company*: a mode now more consciously attempted by modern cultural collectives.

Group coordination

What is eventually clear, however, is that a much more formal and regular division of labour, based not only on professionalization but also on conscious management, corresponds to an effectively new stage in the means of production. In the case of theatre this is especially clear. The 'producer', 'director' or 'manager' emerged when wholly coordinated production not only of the acting but of new staging techniques, including new kinds of design and lighting, was seen as necessary and desirable. The earliest figures of this kind were still actors or writers, but the new role rapidly increased in importance, until by the mid-twentieth century the director could see himself, and was often seen by others, as the central productive figure.

A new division of labour

Yet these were still redistributions of role and authority within working professional companies. The deepest changes came only with the development of the new reproductive technologies. They are most obvious in cinema and television.

First, the new technology required a much more extensive professional specialization. Writers and actors, and then designers, were joined by cameramen, sound recordists, editors and a whole range of people with ancillary skills. At the simplest technical level, the role of a coordinating director became almost inevitable. But then, second, there was a further division of labour, in the installation, maintenance and some forms of operation of the technology itself: electricians, carpenters, logistical staff. These can be said to represent only a development from earlier kinds of craft support, but the general situation was qualitatively new, in that work in this area became indispensable, in the advanced technologies, even though there could still be doubt whether such workers were truly part of the cultural production. It is here that class lines became drawn, often with continuing argument about jobs at or near the point of division.

Printing and 'writing'

The significant test case is that of printers and other 'manual' workers in modern newspaper production. It is firmly asserted, within existing class assumptions, that such workers have no legitimate concern whatever with the content of the cultural production. Printers who refuse to print some particular item in a newspaper are denounced as wreckers, and as a threat to the freedom of the press. What has then happened is a class division, of a stable and organized kind, within cultural production. On one side of the division there are those who 'write', on the other those who 'print'. The former process is seen as cultural production, the latter as merely instrumental.

It is ironic to see the terms of this division being renegotiated as newer technology, such as computer typesetting, makes the technical division unnecessary or redundant. But whatever happens to particular processes, it remains a general condition of modern cultural technology that it both requires social forms of production and yet, within this, under specific economic conditions, imposes not only a professional but a class division of labour.

Ownership

Specific economic conditions are a further decisive factor in the new reproductive technologies. One kind of individual artist can own his immediate means of production, though he is then typically involved with others, in market or other relationships, in distribution. A professional company, in favourable circumstances, can own or lease its immediate means of production, and deal relatively directly with its public, while its technical means are relatively simple. But in the advanced technologies, up to our own time, it has been almost impossible for working companies to have direct access to their relevant means of production, and a third form of the division of labour then appears, and in capitalist conditions becomes stable and regular. Beyond professional specialization, and beyond the internal class division within social forms of cultural production, there is this ultimately controlling form of ownership and management, within which the other forms have to operate. Every kind of cultural and productive worker, within the highly capitalized systems of these advanced technologies, becomes an employee of owners or managers who need not be directly concerned with cultural production at all.

This is of course never only an economic relationship. Wholly dependent on one or one type of owner or controller of his means of production, the cultural worker in these technologies is in a radically different set of social relations from those of the individual producer or earlier type of company, and fundamental questions of cultural autonomy and purpose are raised in quite new ways. Moreover, social relations of this new type have themselves passed through significant stages. The common early situation of the individual capitalist owner, or proprietary family, was replaced, within conditions of more organized markets, by various forms of combine arrangements, at a significantly greater distance from the immediate producers and in their internal corporative organization exhibiting a crucial new layer of professional management of production, which quickly became dominant. Such combines are still common, in various forms, but further problems of capitalization, marketing and integration of production have led to the widespread appearance of the conglomerate, within which ownership and control of the means of cultural production become a sector within the wider ownership and control of a much wider (non-cultural) productive and financial area. The conglomerate is indeed becoming typical of technologically advanced cultural production in the advanced capitalist economies, and its theoretical importance, in this context, is that it is at once dominant in modern cultural production and yet, in its determining forms, radically separate from it; its 'purpose' (cf. page 67) now primarily elsewhere.

The consequent transformation of the situation of the cultural producer, in some of the major modern cultural forms, is clearly of great importance. It is a familiar case of one of the basic contradictions of modern capitalism, in which increasingly socialized forms of production are defined and limited by privately appropriated forms of ownership and control. There is a comparable contradiction in those other cases where the form of appropriation is directly or indirectly by the State, and socialized forms of production are in practice controlled by an imposed management. It can be seen that problems of this kind are inseparable from major developments in cultural means of production, and especially the major reproductive technologies. But this does not mean that the technologies *imposed* the social forms, which have indeed followed the main lines of general social and economic power. Even within the necessarily centralized and high-capital technologies, other social forms are possible: for example, public ownership of the means of production combined with leasing of these means to independent (rather than employed) companies and groups.

Alternative forms

For what we have also to notice is that in some of the most advanced technologies – in one sector video and new kinds of print reproduction; in another sector common-carrier types of transmission, such as cable and teletext – opportunities for some significant recovery of direct access to their means of production, for some modern kinds of cultural producer, either exist or can be realistically looked for. In the technical changes of our own period, new forms of access, and new social forms of collective cultural production, are in fact being intensively explored. These are still only marginally emergent, and are under great pressure from the dominant forms of developed capitalist and state-capitalist modes, which often have the additional advantage that they effectively control the production and the directions of the newest technologies. Yet at least it can be said that the long and complex history of the relations between cultural producers and their material means of production has not ended, but is still open and active.

5 Identifications

We can go a long way in the sociology of culture by studying cultural institutions, formations and means of production. But at some point we are bound to stop and ask if what we are studying, however important it may be in its own terms, is sufficiently central to its presumed subject. We now have the sociology, it is sometimes said, but where is the art?

This is usually a reasonable question. It is true that there is one unreasonable apparent form of it, which is intended, really, to halt the whole inquiry. Certain sociological facts and considerations are rather hastily admitted, usually in a received and well-worn form, and some minor place is reserved for them. But then, we understand, the real work can begin; we go to 'the works of art themselves'.

'The works of art themselves'

Of course, as an everyday decision, something like this is possible. We can and often should stop reasoning about art, and go instead to look at a painting, listen to some music, read a poem. But this is quite different from that *conceptual* shift, in which we are invited to break off the sociological inquiry and move, not to some specific attention, but to a generalized category with its presumed internal rules. It is the difference between a necessary empirical shift, when reasoning is taken across to one of its presumed objects and must take the full strain of the encounter, and a deceptive (because falsely generalized) empiricism, in which certain kinds of attention to certain presumptively autonomous objects are held to be justified and protected by the terms of an unargued immediacy. It is one thing to leave sociological analysis and instead read a poem; it is quite another to leave socio-cultural analysis and forthwith adopt a socio-cultural category whose forms and terms ought, precisely, to be the object of analysis.

For 'the works of art themselves' is of course a category, and not some neutral objective description. It is a socio-cultural category of the highest importance, but just because of this it cannot be empirically presumed. Consider only the very diverse practices it offers to unite or even, in some versions, to make in some sense identical. Radically different manual practices, directed to radically different human senses (over a range, for example, from sight alone to hearing alone), are presumptively encompassed by this single general category. The concept would be difficult enough if it were only at this level, where we say that music, dance, painting, sculpture, poetry, drama, fiction, film have crucial properties in common, which suffice to distinguish them, as a group, from other human practices.

But another level is immediately in question, even as we nominate the group. The case of dance is an obvious example. There are forms of dance which we all admit as forms of art: for example, classical ballet. But then there are other forms where this description does not suggest itself, or might not be admitted if it did: for example, ballroom dancing, which would be normally set down simply as 'a pleasurable social activity' (and as such different from art?).

One early distinction suggests itself: ballet is performed for an audience; ballroom dancing is where we can all join in. But what would then be the case with an exhibition or competition of ballroom dancing? The next distinction suggests itself: ballet is a higher, more developed form of dance, and as such is art, while ballroom dancing is at best only marginally so, and normally not at all so. But then consider folk-dance, ordinarily less developed, formally, than ballet; indeed often no more developed than ballroom dances. Yet folk-dance is regularly presented, in certain kinds of exhibition and performance, as at least a simple kind of art.

Art as performance?

Is this where the earlier distinction returns: that 'art' depends on conscious performance? It clearly takes us some way, but there are still major difficulties. Cave paintings, for example, are now generally and under-standably seen as art, indeed in many of their examples as major art. Yet they are commonly sited in dark and inaccessible places, and we really do not know how often, if at all, they were generally seen, within the period and culture in which they were made. Then take a limiting case: if nobody but the original painter or painters of the great roof bison of Altamira had ever seen this work (and comparable work may still be lying undiscovered), would any of us wish, on our first sight of it, to deny its status as art because it had not been consciously exhibited?

Art as quality?

Is its status then a matter of its superlative material execution? This is obviously crucial, but it will not serve to delimit art; the same criterion, on its own, would distinguish many works of other manual skills and of engineering. Indeed often, and only sometimes rhetorically, we speak of such works as works of art – a particular knife, pot, aeroplane, bridge – but usually with the sense that this is an additional quality, when the primary purpose of the object has been already acknowledged. Meanwhile the category of 'art' is normally and even insistently applied to works which have no other purpose but to be works of art

'Aesthetic' purpose

This definition by purpose, by an in effect autonomous intention, is perhaps the most common modern justification of the category. It commands an entire voculabulary, centred on the specification of the *'aesthetic'*: a work of art is designed for, and/or has, aesthetic properties and effects. In fact 'aesthetic' in this sense is a new term from the late eighteenth century, moving directly in line with the modern specializing generalization of 'the arts' and 'the creative arts', though the qualities it indicates had often previously been described. Because of the interlock of terms – 'aesthetic intention', 'creative arts', 'aesthetic effect' – an effective categorical grouping has indeed been achieved. But then it should be clear, when we see this as a categorical formation rather than an obvious and neutral description, that what passes, often very effectively, as a solution brings in its train some particularly difficult problems.

It can seem relatively easy to categorize 'the aesthetic'. It is usually done by introducing supporting or specifying terms: either general terms like 'beauty' or more particular terms like 'harmony', 'proportion', 'form'. And indeed there can be little doubt that the qualities these terms indicate, as processes and as responses, are very significant and important. Much might be done in the scientific analysis of these processes and responses, many of which are self-evidently material and physical. But whether or not this is done we have a great body of human testimony to the reality of what is being (if still generally) described.

Specialization of the 'aesthetic'

The real problem is not at this level, where the significance of perceptions of colour, form, harmony, rhythm, proportion and so on can be readily confirmed. The intractable problem is the presumed specialization of these 'perceptions' – these processes and responses – to 'works of art'. For it is common to experience similar or comparable perceptions of the human body, of animals and birds, or of trees, flowers and the shapes and colours of land. There is certainly interaction between these and the processes and responses of many arts: many works are derived from or stimulated by them; other works articulate new 'natural' perceptions. But even when we have allowed for this, there is no ready way of defining the category 'art' from these undoubted and general human perceptions, which we are bound to recognize as more widely applicable and thus not reducible to a specialization.

Moreover there are problems of marginal definition. In wholly man-made processes, the 'arts' run through into the

significant areas of dress, ornament, furnishing, decoration, gardening, where many of the same criteria of
beauty, harmony and proportion apply yet where the full
definition as 'art' is usually withheld, within the modern
specialization. At the same time, in a quite different
direction, the 'arts' run through into areas of human
thought and discourse – values, truths, ideas, observations,
reports – where, though the 'aesthetic' perceptions may be
still quite relevant, they cannot be and in practice are not
taken as wholly defining. Most of us want, at times, to speak
of the 'truth' of a work of art as much as, or even more than,
its 'beauty'.

'Art' and 'not art'

The second major problem which follows from the
conventional categorization is of great sociological interest.
It is that within the practices thus selected and grouped
there is a common further delimitation, by value or by
presumed value.

Now of course distinctions between works in the various
practices, in terms of the quality of their professional
execution or, more generally, of some wider values, are
normal and inevitable. But this does not, without forcing,
mean that such distinctions are clear and regular enough to
delimit a category, and especially a category as difficult as
this: that some works in a practice which has been specified
as an art are 'not art' or 'not really art'. Yet whole socio-
cultural theories, of a kind, have been built on this kind of
argument. Thus some novels are 'works of art', but others
are 'pulp fiction', 'commercial trash', 'sub-literature' or
'para-literature', and yet others, between these poles, are
'routine', 'mediocre' or 'lending-library fodder'. We can all
think of examples to which we would apply these

descriptions and be willing to give reasons. The terms are harsher in the more popular arts, but the tendency exists through the whole range.

And what we can then see happening is a hardening of specific judgements into presumptions of classes, based now not only on mixed criteria (for there are held to be cases of 'skilfully executed nonsense' or 'professionally brilliant hokum' as well as of 'clumsy art' or 'raw but authentic artistic power') but also, and crucially, on criteria which are incompatible with the original delimitation by the nature of the practice. Thus a 'bad novel' does everything that the category 'novel' indicates, at the level of generic definition, but then fails to do something else, either in its 'aesthetic process' or in terms of its 'seriousness' or its 'relation to reality' (which, at least explicitly, the original definition had not included).

Moreover, if we bring to this common confusion the elementary historical observation that these presumptive classes of 'art' and 'sub-art' or 'non-art' tend to shift (all novels, once, would have been in the downgrading classes; particular classes of novel, for example 'science fiction', move from one side of the divide to another, or are straddled across it; cinema films are 'commercial popular culture' but then some films are 'high art'), we become more and more certain that we must refuse that beguiling invitation to leave aside 'sociological categories' and move to 'the works of art themselves'. Moreover we must refuse by a criterion often rhetorically invoked in these doubtful positions; by the criterion of the strictest intellectual coherence and rigour.

The social processes of 'art'

For what really becomes clear, as we review these effective categorizations, with all their problems and loose ends, is that the move away from the 'sociological' is precisely the move we cannot make. While these difficult categorizations, either in their most serious and sustained forms, or in their commonly received popular forms, retain or attempt to retain their position above society – above the historical socio-material process or the full, undelimited cultural process – they have to be seen not only as intellectually unsatisfactory but as, in themselves, disguised social processes. Everything is then to be gained by their serious recognition as social processes; moreover as social processes of a highly significant and valuable kind. The attempt to distinguish 'art' from other, often closely related, practices is a quite extraordinarily important historical and social process. The attempt to distinguish 'aesthetic' from other kinds of attention and response is, as a historical and social process, perhaps even more important. The attempt to distinguish between good, bad and indifferent work in specific practices is, when made in full seriousness and without the presumption of privileged classes and habits, an indispensable element of the central social process of conscious human production. And when we see these attempts as themselves social processes, we can continue the inquiry, instead of cutting it short.

'Social' and 'sociological'

But first a note of caution. Some of the social processes we are now coming to consider can be seriously reduced in significance if we take the 'sociological' emphasis in too narrow (and unfortunately common) a sense. There are important parts of these processes to which this narrow sense is relevant. The modern distinction between 'high culture' and 'popular culture', for example, is impenetrable without the closest consideration of the shifting structures of social class. The categorical transitions from 'court' and 'peasant' to 'aristocratic' and 'folk' art reveal directly, in their terms, social associations of a determinate kind which 'high' and 'popular', in significantly blurring ways, still partly retain. The direct application of normal sociological categories can take us much of the way in these relatively explicit, but also relatively local and shifting, cases. Yet in some of the most fundamental areas of the enquiry, we find ourselves involved with societal processes which can be said to precede some senses of 'sociology'. This is especially so in that area of cultural groupings, selections and emphases, which run through (though of course are not unaffected by) otherwise radically different social orders.

Lukács on specificity

Consider, for example, the bold attempt by Lukács (1969) to define the specificity of art by distinguishing three phases of human practice: the 'practical', the 'magico-religious', the 'aesthetic'. Here the 'practical' relates to the satisfaction of perceived human needs, within historically determinate social and material conditions. The 'magico-religious' relates to the encounter with perceived human limits (some of them, as seen by others, historically determinate, but to almost all there and then, and to many always, intractable) and the consequent making of images or stories in that distinguishable area. These remain 'magico-religious' while they are offered as, in this area, objectively real, transcendent and demanding belief. The way is then clear for a specifying definition of the 'aesthetic', which is not the practical satisfaction of a determinate need, but which is also not offered as objectively real and demanding ('magico-religious') belief; its images are closed and real in themselves.

Now I have never thought that this bold scheme works, in the categorical terms in which it is offered (I have summarized these, partly in my own vocabulary; for the full argument see Lukács, 1969). Too many processes and objects from the 'practical' and 'magico-religious' phases come to demand inclusion in the 'aesthetic' phase. Too many 'aesthetic' processes and objects overlap, in practice, with the 'practical' and the magico-religious'. It is indeed the relative integrity of these phases, in certain periods of human practice, which allows us to see certain subsequent specializations, in periods of altered general practice, as historical rather than categorical facts (and the theory of Lukács, in terms, as idealist rather than historical-materialist).

Yet the emphasis he is attempting does not then seem irrelevant. For there is indeed an observable general tendency (however deeply complicated by historical and cultural diversity) to distinguish and to value kinds of work which meet no immediate and manifest need, of an everyday practical kind, and which are at least not necess-arily taken as evidence of some metaphysical or non-human dimension of reality. Indeed this is so clear that I sometimes wonder why so much effort usually goes into attempting to prove it. Such work can serve societal purposes, of the deepest kind: not as food, or as shelter, or as tools, but as 'recognitions' (both new and confirming marks) of people and kinds of people in places and kinds of place, and indeed often as more than this, as 'recognitions' of a physical species in a practically shared physical universe, with its marvellously diverse interactions of senses, forces, potentials. So deep a human interest – in the renewed and renewable means of recognition, self-recognition and identity – can be practised over a very wide range, from the most collective to the most individual forms. In some of its farthest reaches it has often to be contrasted with routinized or habituated forms of perception and recognition, which can then be falsely specialized as the 'merely social'. What matters is the evidence, in many thousands of processes and objects, of constant human practice in this real dimension, necessarily overlapping and interacting with other kinds of practice but never simply reducible to them.

Specificity and specificities

It is from the range and power of this kind of human activity and attention, which we find in so many different kinds of social order and in so many different historical periods, that the impulse to categorize 'the aesthetic' begins and seems justified. Yet just because it is so general and common a process, finding its means and occasions and objects in such diverse ways, and again and again interpenetrating with many of the most practical or most ideological activities, it cannot reasonably be abstracted to one exclusive set of practices or one exclusive intention or set of intentions. On the other hand this does not mean that everything, including the most specifically artistic and most specifically aesthetic processes, has to be dissolved into some indiscriminate general social or cultural practice. It is simply that the necessary distinctions are not to be found at the level of categorical separation but rather at the level where they are in fact produced, which is that of both general and specific cultural and social orders.

The arts as social forms

The distinctions between art and non-art, or between aesthetic and other intentions and responses, as well as those more flexible distinctions by which elements of a process, or intentions and responses, are seen, in real cases, as predominant or subordinate, can then be seen as they historically are: as variable social forms within which the relevant practices are perceived and organized. Thus the distinctions are not eternal verities, or supra-historical categories, but actual elements of a kind of social organization.

It is interesting that such distinctions are most clearly and most confidently made in relatively complex and highly specialized societies. Indeed there is much evidence to suggest that the distinctions are most actively sought in periods of growing secularization, when the habit of referring all practices, finally, to some central faith and purpose, is loosening or has been lost. But forms of the distinctions, which are always also emphases of importance, are in fact widespread, in many diverse social orders. Indeed the first deep form of the social organization of art is, in this sense, the social perception of art itself.

The signals of art

Such perception is always practical, whether or not it is followed by theoretical reasoning. A vast and ordinarily unnoticed area of the history of the arts is the development of systems of social signals that what is now to be made available is to be regarded as art. These systems are very diverse, but between them they constitute the practical social organization of that first deep cultural form in which certain arts are grouped, emphasized and distinguished.

The most common kinds of signal are those of *occasion* and *place*. These are at their simplest, because at their most specialized, in relatively complex and secular societies. The signal of an art gallery is an especially obvious case. It is a place specialized and designated for looking at painting or drawing or sculpture as art. This signal is so established and conventional that it hardly has to be noticed. Indeed the gallery can be seen as if it were only (which of course it is also) a mere technical device for the objects to be displayed. Yet consider the difference when we see a drawing or a painting on an ordinary street or house wall. There is an immediate question as to why it is there: is it what some vandal has done, or some unauthorized dauber, or some impulsive and frustrated artist, or some new policy of bringing art into the streets? We may often be sure that we can judge by the quality of the drawing or painting, but there are always at least some cases in which our uncertainty is deepened by the absence of the expected signal, that it is or is not intended to be art.

This situation has many ironic effects. Some artists become so resentful of the conventionalities that come with the signal – the imposition, as it is said, of a merely 'arty' atmosphere – that they consciously take their work to other, 'more normal' places. Usually, in doing so, they set up *alternative signals*: that this tent, this stretch of street, this canteen, this waiting-room, is where this different kind of artist wants his work to be seen. Or the signal can be both accepted and questioned. In a famous recent case, someone said: 'If I'd seen this pile of bricks on the side of the road I'd never have thought it was art'. 'But now you've seen it in an art gallery, do you think it is art?', someone else asked. And then there were different answers, from those listening to the exchange. 'Well I suppose it must be, if they think so.' 'Somebody must think so, if they paid that much for it.' 'It may be to them, but it isn't to me; it's still just a pile of bricks.' 'Why do they put this rubbish on show, instead of some real art?'

At the margins of the practice, and especially in unfamiliar kinds of work, these variable reactions between the signal and actual responses are quite common. But over a much wider range than we usually recognize, the signal works without question, because it is a conventional way of answering what would otherwise be (and may still really be) difficult or impossibly difficult questions, about the nature of the work and about the appropriate kind of response.

Signal systems

Consider another case: that of dramatic performance. For some centuries this has been primarily signalled by a specialized place: a theatre. The signal system of advertised time of performance, arrangement of seating, raising of curtains and so on is especially coherent. In one style of play, what happens within these signals is very consciously made to resemble, as far as possible, what happens in everyday rooms and everyday behaviour and conversation; yet the signals hold, this is still a play. If the same play is put on television (as a television production, and not as simple transmission from a theatre) other kinds of signal, mainly titles, including keywords like 'play' or 'theatre', are employed. But there is then sometimes an interesting area of overlap, where the style is employed for what is taken to be other material: the 'drama-documentary', the 'dramatic reconstruction'. This can lead to a confusion of signals. There have been long and fierce arguments, inside television, as to whether, when a play is 'directly based on a real-life case', there should be further signals, indicating divergence from the expected norm. But these are significantly difficult to decide on. In which direction should the signal point? That this is, after all, 'only a play'? That 'though it looks like a real-life case, it is really not'? That 'all these things really happened, and can be taken as true'?

Simple conventional signals depend, of course, on relatively stable forms, and on relatively settled places and occasions. This conservatism, however, often leads to conscious revolt, by artists with different purposes, who then either confuse or even omit the known signals. There is the famous case of the radio dramatization of Wells's *War of the Worlds*, which, within a confusion of signals, such as use of the convention of radio news reports, was quite widely received as an 'actuality' account of an alien invasion. There is also the interesting case of the experimental company which 'staged' 'dramatic situations', such as a fierce marital row, in restaurants, while appearing to be ordinary customers. Here the total absence of signals led to every kind of confusion, but its point was a testing of the function of such signals: did the normal 'framing' of such situations, which at the restaurant table might follow word by word and action by action the scene of a play, inhibit or qualify the responses of 'others'/'an audience'?

The sociology of signal systems

The signal systems by which 'art' is indicated have then a complex sociology. There are many *integrated systems* which become fully institutional: theatre, art gallery, concert hall. These integrated systems are in general a function of specialization: distinct arts in distinct places at distinct times. Modern broadcasting systems, carrying all these arts but carrying also news, discussion, transmitted non-artistic events and 'factual programmes', have quite different problems, mainly solved, at an initial level, by conscious internal titling and description.

But as we go back to much earlier periods, the signal systems are complex in different ways again. Consider English medieval popular drama, indicated, generally, not so much by a place (a theatre) as by an occasion, usually the festival of Corpus Christi. Performance was in the streets, but many of the normal dramatic signals – costume, effects, rudimentary scene – were given. Typically also, however, there was common use of preliminary direct address, to indicate both the subject and the fact of its performance. This function of 'prologue' (and of 'epilogue' or in the medieval case concluding homily) continued into much later drama. It is on the borderline between a true signal, indicating the nature of the coming activity and establishing specific relations within which it is intended to occur, and that type of signal which is not preparatory or externally indicative but is integrated *within* the form of a work: a type which we can distinguish as conventions, and which is so fundamentally important that it will be separately discussed, below.

Meanwhile the borderline case is important in understanding the complexity of primary signal systems. Thus, before medieval drama went into the streets as part of a religious festival, less developed kinds of dramatization of several of the same events – key moments in the Christian history of the world – had been performed in churches, and some of the very earliest of these – the *Quem quaeritis?* episodes of the encounters after the resurrection – had been performed *within* religious services. What signals were then being given? The use of 'dramatic' means to 'enact' the presence and the meeting of Christ is surely not to be taken, at this stage, as a signal of 'art', in the modern sense.

But can we then be quite sure that at a later stage, when the same kind of performance has been taken out of the service and then out of the church, the signal is unambiguously to 'art'? The fact surely is that, within any specific culture, the nature of the signals, and of the shared signifying system within which they must operate, is radically connected with the social organization of a very wide area of perceived reality.

It is often the tensions and shifts of such systems, in periods of significant change, that show this most clearly. Thus we have to say of medieval popular drama that the sense of ritual 'presence', of the kind still indicated by the formalized words and movements of the mass, has significantly changed, but may in some new combination of signals be still to some extent active, in ways that it is clearly not in later forms and systems. Thus it is significant that in a more secular drama (affected also by some of the emphases of Protestantism) the formerly habitual direct dramatic presentation of God the Father or Jesus Christ became prohibited or unthinkable. In an even more secular society, and one in which the signals of 'drama' (meaning now not 'presence' but 'representation') were more generally organized and familiar, just these once 'normal' but then prohibited dramatic presentations have reappeared.

Signals in Greek drama

When there is this kind of historical development of a signal system it is important that it should not be read back in the exclusive terms of later signals. It is equally important not to reduce intermediate stages to the earliest terms. The case of classicial Greek drama is especially relevant. It is important, when reading the plays, not to overlook the specific signal system within which they were performed. The performances were part of a religious

festival, the City Dionysia, in the Theatre of Dionysus.
Each day's performances began with a sacrifice and
libations; the priest of Dionysus sat in the centre front of
the audience; the image of the god, normally kept in the
temple adjacent to the theatre, had been carried in
procession and placed in the theatre; in the centre of the
orchestra was an altar. All these were signals of a religious
kind, framing the performances in culturally specific ways.
Yet, while this function must be emphasized, we must not
overlook some new kinds of signal. This drama is often now
confused with, or even rendered back to, types of religious
ritual in which some of its elements indeed originated. But
in fact the new signals were crucial. The figures were not
priests and worshippers, but actors and chorus in front of
an audience. The reiterated formalities of ritual had been
replaced by the specific and (even on the same themes)
consciously variable compositions of words and actions by
individual dramatists. The performed plays, and the
acting, were in conscious competition for prizes.

None of these signals indicate ritual; they indicate
'drama', in our general sense of art. Yet this signal system
indicating 'art' occurred, with sufficient effect, within a still
functioning signal system of another kind. Was the work
then a cross between drama and ritual? Not at all. In the
performances themselves the dramatic signals were dominant; in the organization of the festival the religious signals
were dominant.

Complexity of signals

This kind of complexity of signal, directly related to the
complexities of a specific social and cultural order, is
indeed quite common. It is only from some insistence,
within some other social and cultural order, that signals
should always be singular in dimension – indicating 'pure
art' and the 'purely aesthetic' in manifestly specializing,

and then both emphasizing and excluding, ways – that these historical and sociological complexities are resisted. Yet even within such an order there are enough complexities of signals, of a different kind – the 'command performance', in honour of the already honoured; the 'private view' – who has been invited to look in this privileged way?; the 'special performance', for an audience of a socially selected type – to remind us of the always variable – historically and culturally variable – social organization and social function of art.

Internal signals

Many signal systems, as we have seen, operate directly, indeed necessarily, within the terms of their more general social and cultural order. But it is also a crucial fact in the development of art that some kinds of signal become internalized, or are indeed quite internally developed, within art forms. Moreover some, indeed many, of these become effective over a wide cultural range and through different historical periods. This is where a narrowly sociological interpretation, which is relevant in the cases of signalled occasions, signalled places and modes of assembly, and of course specialized formal institutions, can reach its limits, or, more dangerously, override them.

Thus narrative and the portrait and dramatic performance are in their origins manifestly socially conditioned, and in their development (we shall be looking at some cases) still radically socially conditioned. But at the same time there are effective continuities, and forms of what it often seems reasonable to call internal, 'systemic' development, which make any discrete assignment of 'forms' to specific social orders at best difficult, at worst quite misleading.

Yet when this is realized there seems occasion for that familiar intellectual move, by which the 'history' of each art form is written as it were independently. What 'happens' to prose narrative, or to the sonnet, seems and indeed is sufficiently substantial and interesting, historically, to be written as if it were in effect autonomous. In fact without these specialized histories our relevant knowledge would be quite inadequate. It is not such histories, but the ideology usually underlying or deduced from them, that must be most critically scrutinized. For we do not have to look far, in any such history, to find the displaced social conditions from which the move to 'autonomy' is often no more than a kind of compositional emphasis. Indeed, in many such histories, the social conditions are directly introduced, indeed as introductions, or can be said to hover, as what is called 'background'. It is not in such cases that the central theoretical problem is posed. It is when an ideology underlies or is deduced from them that we see a conventional avoidance of the theoretical problem, by a manifest eclecticism or by *ad hoc* rules of reference or relevance.

'Formalist' versus 'sociological'

The real theoretical problem, if initially in a very curious definition, was indicated by the modern schools of Formalism, and it is from that source that the most significant modern arguments have flowed. It is unfortunate that these were confused, at an early stage, by crude classifications of two generally opposed positions as '*formalist*' and '*sociological*'. The effects of this confusion are still damaging and widespread.

Yet we can see why various formalists chose 'sociological' as a contemptuous description of their real or presumed adversaries. What 'sociological' then meant was either concentration on the general conditions of a practice, to the partial or total neglect of the practice itself; or, more immediately, appropriation of works in terms of their manifest or presumed social content, which was then assimilated to social content deduced from quite other sites, thus obliterating the most specific (and then it was said, the most formal) properties of the work or kind of work.

Since both these things had happened, the challenge was necessary and salutary. But it is characteristic of simple formalism that it tended merely to reverse the priorities of its adversaries, and a more complex formalism soon found itself engaged with just the problems of social and cultural form which the best 'sociological' work had been defining and trying to solve.

Formalist analysis and 'forms'

For what formalist analysis revealed, often much more sharply than in any earlier kind of analysis, was the specific composition of *forms*. On the other hand, in its simplest early work, it described this crucial fact of composition in terms of *devices*, on characteristically technicist assumptions. An example will make the necessary distinctions clear.

Soliloquy

The soliloquy in drama can be described as a 'device. It has first to be distinguished from single direct address, which is still public in mode. An example is the Ma¬hevill prologue in Marlowe's *The Jew of Malta*:

> I come not, I,
> To read a lecture here in Britain,
> But to present the tragedy of a Jew.

The soliloquy, by contrast, can be initially defined, as in dictionaries, as a man speaking aloud *to himself*. But this cannot be reduced to some naturalistic explanation, of a character happening to find himself alone. It is a deliberate compositional element of the drama: a mode of dramatic speech. At the same time it cannot be reduced to the kind of device indicated by the definition 'speaking to himself'. Indeed it cannot be fully analysed, even as a device, until its full situation and content are included. For example we can distinguish between the following uses:

(i) for the expression of *secret* thoughts, which other characters must not know. An example is Edmund in *King Lear*, I.ii.182–5:

> a brother noble
> Whose nature is so far from doing harms
> That he suspects none; on whose foolish honesty
> My practices ride easy! I see the business.

(ii) for speech *to the self as to another*, in a form of self presentation. An example is Faustus in Marlowe's *Doctor Faustus*, I, i.

> Settle thy studies, Faustus, and begin
> To sound the depth of that thou wilt profess.

In the same play, V, ii, the same speech form is used at the beginning of Faustus' final soliloquy –

> Ah Faustus
> Now hast thou but one bare hour to live

– but changed at the crisis of his terror:

> Oh, I'll leap up to my God.

(iii) for the expression of *inner conflict*, the process rather than the product of thinking. An example is Hamlet in *Hamlet*, II.ii.585 ff:

> O, vengeance!
> Why, what an ass am I . . .
> About, my brains . . .

(iv) for the expression of certain ultimate conflicts, in *an enforced indirection of address*, where, in a given situation, adequate speech to any particular other is not available. An example is in *Hamlet*, III.i.56, where by contrast with the other soliloquies based on the pronoun 'I' – I.ii.129; IV.iv.33 – the soliloquy is written impersonally, and the crucial pronouns are 'we' and 'us':

> and by a sleep to say we end
> The heart-ache . . .

In further analysis, there are complex combinations of these and perhaps other modes.

And then what can still, in case (i), or as in the related method of the 'aside', be called a device, is in the more developed and complex cases an innovating series of formal elements which can be shown to be inseparable from new conceptions of personality and new senses of the limits and contradictions of available social relations. In this inseparability, the soliloquy is at once a new compositional mode and a new kind of content, and these, taken together, are indispensable evidence of that most central of cultural processes: the formation of specific forms within a general form.

Thus, initiated and developed by individual writers, within an already shared practice and form, the soliloquy became a *convention* in the course of establishing relations with audiences who learned to accept its modes: at the simplest level, the convention of accepting that a man speaking on a stage in full hearing of an audience cannot be heard by another actor who has moved a few paces away; at more complex levels, that he is not even addressing the audience, but is being overheard by or is in some sense speaking for them.

These new and subtle modes and relationships were in themselves developments in social practice, and are fundamentally connected with the discovery, *in dramatic form*, of new and altered social relationships, perceptions of self and others, complex alternatives of private and public thought. It is then true that what has been discovered, and can later be analysed, in the form can be shown to be relatively associated with a much wider area of social practice and social change. New conceptions of the autonomous or relatively autonomous individual, new senses of the tensions between such an individual and an assigned or expected social role, evident in other kinds of contemporary discourse but evident also in analytic history of the major social changes of this precise period, are then in clear relation with the 'device'

But it is not necessary to explain the device as their consequence, taking first the sociology and then the form. This may often appear to be the order of events, but it is often also clear that the formal innovation is a true and integral element of the changes themselves: an articulation, by technical discovery, of changes in consciousness which are themselves forms of consciousness of change. Thus to analyse the soliloquy in English Renaissance drama is necessarily, first, a matter of formal analysis, but not as a way of denying or making irrelevant a social analysis; rather as a new and technically rigorous kind of social analysis of *this* social practice.

We can then see the point at which formal analysis necessarily challenges previously limited or displaced kinds of social analysis. For while social analysis is confined to the society which, as it were, *already* exists, in completed ways, before the cultural practice begins, it is not only that analyses made elsewhere are simply applied to actual works, imposing on them only the most general consider-ations and missing or neglecting other elements of their composition. It is also that actual evidence of the general socio-cultural process, in one of its significant practices, is not even looked for, though it is in fact abundant. This is the point of transition for a sociology of culture, to include, as a major emphasis, the *sociology of forms*.

Structuralist analysis

Yet it is still, at this stage, only a partial sociology. Indeed, from its sources in formalist analysis, it is often pulled back to quite other theoretical orbits. Thus it can be insisted that the formal composition, the formal structure, of narrative or drama reveals fundamental forms of social relationship, but at a level which can then be taken as determining, with the consequence that different forms of narrative or drama are seen *only* as variations of a fundamental form, and are explained as the result of internal, 'systemic' developments, in a way that makes other kinds of social change, or even their own internal history, as history, irrelevant.

This has been the general position of *structuralism*, which then offers a theory of social relations which is in effect alternative to all other accounts of what are taken to be social relations. The basic cultural structures, either exhibiting their variations, or 'evolving' entirely within their own forms, are either independent or relatively autonomous from other social history and practice, or are even its deep, generally determining forms. Encouraged by earlier neglect of this significant formal and structural evidence, this position comes to override all other kinds of knowledge and analysis, by the simple move of declaring it, *a priori*, irrelevant. This may race the blood but it does not usually survive much actual inquiry.

Genetic structuralism

A more plausible version tries to hold structural determination and relative autonomy at a more protected, deliberately specializing level. Thus *genetic structuralism*, as in Goldmann (1970), puts a decisive emphasis on the evolution of forms, analysing their building and dissolution, by contrast with the idea of permanent forms which simply exhibit variations. But though it then relates some of these forms to actual historical transitions, of a general kind, it insists not only that these relations are purely formal (they are not, in any sense, correspondences of content), but that only some such relations are significant: a position defended by declaring, again *a priori*, that it is only at a certain ('major') level that such relations exist, and that all other available work and relations are 'ephemeral' and therefore insignificant and negligible. The questions are indeed very complex, and there need be no difficulty in agreeing that some forms and relations are much more important than others. But any form of *a priori* exclusion of knowable areas of a culture is as unacceptable as the more evidently arbitrary exclusion of 'history' or other 'peripheral' concerns. It is the condition of any adequate sociology of culture that it is open, in principle and practice, to all possible evidence.

Conditions of practice

Yet one can see why such emphases arose. There was often such a gap between the most general social history and sociology and these highly specific analyses of form that it was tempting to draw a line, if only to discourage the building of paper bridges or even more airy constructions.

The description of this line as 'relative autonomy' was, in some of its forms, a positive advance, in emphasizing the specificity of a practice; a specificity that indeed needs to be granted to *all* practices. What was really missing was an adequate theoretical account of the *conditions of a practice*, for it is in these conditions that a specificity can be affirmed, and yet the inevitable relations between different practices explored. This will be more generally discussed below, in relation to the social history of dramatic forms.

Conditions of the soliloquy

But we can take the argument one step further by returning to discussion of the soliloquy. If we put, as it were in one column, the (differentiated) formal characteristics of the soliloquy, and, as it were in another column, the general social changes in self-conceptions of the individual and in relations between individuals in this new sense and their assigned or expected social roles, we can make some significant correlations.

The form of direct public address, by a single speaker, is evidently congruent with a stable distribution of authority and occasion to speak: a systematic distribution of speaking and listening roles. The simplest expressions of secret thoughts, while incongruent with such a distribution at its ordinary social level, is nevertheless congruent within dramatic forms, as a device of plot, to make intrigue explicit, or as that kind of self-exposure which in its own way confirms the normal public discourse. But all the other forms of 'self-expression' go beyond these received terms. The most obvious case is the expression of inner conflict, where the prepared positions and the assigned actions are put in question not only as a rhetorical form – as objections or hesitations to be answered or overcome – but as a substantial and continuing process, in which this person must decide for himself or indeed cannot decide. The rhetorical form of speaking to the self as to another is similarly transformed when there is a new and strongly felt openness to the question of what the self might *become*, as distinct from what in received terms it is and must be. Each of these developments is directly related to new valuations of individuality, and to new possibilities of self-development and practical change and mobility.

But then they are still questioning forms. The full social terms of such consciousness are not yet regularly available. Thus they are characteristically composed as a man speaking to himself, but, because the development is general and widespread, as a man speaking to himself in these special circumstances: beyond immediately available and confirmed social relations but within newly available dramatic relations: to an indirect or overhearing audience, and in some extreme cases not 'to an audience' at all but in a form of speech which offers to go beyond these still relatively public relations, to the new situation of an individual speaking, as it were silently, with other individuals.

The complexity of these modes then goes beyond matters of correlation. What is being newly attempted and composed is, in varying degrees, itself experimental: part of the general change and search, in its actual processes. It is in this sense that we have to see its dependence on the specific conditions of the practice. Within the complex possibilities of drama as a multivocal form these new kinds of univocal speech can be in one sense embedded, in another sense protected. The most innovatory uses can seem only minor developments from known forms. And this was itself possible only in the conditions of a new kind of audience, within new kinds of theatre, no longer formally defined by the terms, places and occasions of an extra-dramatic authority, but socially mixed and socially mobile within an expanding urban society, served by its own characteristic forms of commercial-enterprise theatres and specializing professional dramatists.

It was in this intrinsically mixed and mobile cultural situation, at a broad but heterogeneous level of popular participation, that, still under risk and under the pressure of received authorities, new kinds of speech, which were also new forms of what could now in these ways be publicly spoken, were intensively explored and often intensely achieved. Thus it was above all in drama that the otherwise general processes of change in conceptions of the self and society were articulated and realized. The ways in which the same changes entered the written single poem or philosophical discourse or narrative are quite different, and of a less powerful kind. For it was above all in the conditions of dramatic practice that these exploratory and still uncertain relations could be practically composed: in the speech forms, most evidently, but also in the fertile complex of shifting relations between the multivocal and the univocal, and between the man speaking in a role and the man speaking as and for himself.

It is in cases like this, of formally identifiable modes and technical procedures, both carrying and exploring a range of known, changing and newly possible social relations, that we find the most interesting examples of those internalized and internally developed signal systems – necessarily in relation with but not always determined by more general and external signal systems – which, as they become working conventions, add a whole area of new evidence to the sociology of cultural practice. We can now, in some more sustained examples, look again at the two kinds of system or form, and at the practical relations between them.

6 Forms

It is clear that certain forms of social relationship are deeply embodied in certain forms of art. It will be useful to look at some actual examples in the case of drama, where we have a long record of specific major forms, in radically different social orders.

We have first to recognize that there can be no absolute separation between those social relationships which are evident or discoverable as the immediate conditions of a practice – the signalled places, occasions and terms of specifically indicated types of cultural activity – and those which are so embedded within the practice, as particular formal articulations, that they are at once social and formal, and can in one kind of analysis be treated as relatively autonomous. The point is especially clear in the earliest historical example, that of the classical Greek tragic drama.

Greek tragedy

Some conditions of this practice have already been described, notably the placing of competitive dramatic performances within a religious festival. It was argued that within this complex social situation, there was an inevitable complexity of 'religious' and 'dramatic' signals, but that while within the organization of the festival the religious signals were dominant, within the actual performances the dramatic signals were dominant. By 'dominant', here, we do not mean excluding or exclusive; the presence, although subordinated, of the other signals is characteristic. But what we have then to examine, at a level much deeper than any ordinary specification of form, is the social articulation of the dramatic, 'drama' itself, at this stage of its relation to pre-dramatic activity.

The historical evidence is complex and incomplete, but some main points can be reasonably assumed. First, there was a known pre-dramatic form, the *dithyramb* or choric hymn, which in fact was still performed (also competitively) at the same festival. Second, there was a limited series of known innovations, of a formal kind, which together constituted a new general form: (i) the innovation of dialogue between a single figure and the (rest of the) chorus; (ii) the innovation of dialogue, now in a more developed sense, between this figure and a second figure (the second actor); (iii) the addition of a third actor. In its mature form, this new 'drama' then consisted of a chorus, with a chorus-leader who was one form of the originally emergent single figure; a protagonist (first actor) who was the more developed form of this same figure; two other (and no more) actors; and attendant mutes. The chorus sang and danced, in one way as in the dithyramb but also in new ways since it was now in deliberate relations with the actors. The chorus-leader additionally used a mode between speech and song, in transitions between the choral singing and the actors' dialogue; his local form ranged from simple indications to a form of dialogue in itself. The actors spoke (in formal metres); they were masked; they shared, between the three of them, all the speaking parts (often seven or eight 'individual characters'). At one or more climaxes, one of the actors sang (as in one of the first innovations) in interaction with the chorus.

The effect of the innovations was of course momentous. By development and imitation (including further innovations, such as in much later periods the extension of the number of actors until there was one to each 'character', and internal reorganizations of emphasis, such as the marginalization of the chorus until it became little more than a musical interlude, and its eventual total exclusion) this new and active specific form became the ground of a general and indeed universal form, which was extensively practised in quite different social orders and practical conditions. Thus a new formal element – that of acted dialogue between individuals – can be traced from its emergence within a specific general form to its emergence as an autonomous general form within which (and now setting their own formal limits) further specific forms were developed.

A new general form

This is an outstanding case of a highly conditioned specific form, of a deep kind, which became, as it were, a quite general cultural property, in the end belonging more to the sociology of our species, at a certain level of cultural development, than to the specific sociology of a given society at a certain place and time. There are other major cases of this kind, which are less well recorded but otherwise no less important: choral singing itself; formal dance; formal narrative; portrait statues; isolated paintings. All are necessary reminders of a decisive level of human societal development, of a general and cumulative kind, which has markedly longer (and often in effect permanent) phases and rhythms than the specific conditions of practice of any particular society or period. Yet these markedly longer phases and rhythms – these deepest forms – can no more be abstracted from general social development than they can be reduced to merely local conditions. The case of acted dialogue between individuals bears precisely on this point.

For what is evident in classical Greek drama is the emergence of this element in precisely controlled relations with other formal elements, and the emergence of its appropriate mode – composed and rehearsed speech – in precisely controlled relations with other modes. The moment of such emergence is then sociologically precise. It was the interaction, and only in that respect the transformation, of a received form (choral singing) with new formal elements which, in their new emphasis, embodied different social relations. The choral song was still a deeply collective mode, though as it moved towards competitive performance and then in part away from an otherwise embedded (religious) occasion, the level of its collectivity was already altering. The emergence of the single figure in deliberate and evident relations to the chorus was compatible with pre-dramatic modes, notably the priest (including the priest as representing the god) in formal relations with a body of worshippers. Yet it contained also elements of compatibility with the dramatic mode, as these relations became deliberately acted. But it was then mainly in the emergence of the *second* figure, making possible relatively independent relations between named separate figures, that the crucial move to what we now recognize as drama was made; the emergence of the third figure obviously took this further.

Specific limits of the Greek form

Yet, within this specific form, the emergence stopped at this point. What later seemed an obvious move – so obvious as to be naturalized as a merely technical distribution of roles, with one actor to each separate figure – was not made. This was not some 'abstention', for practical reasons. It was a clear mark of *the nature and the limits of individuation within this still partly collective form*: a separation of a limited number of individual figures from a maintained collective emphasis; some figures separated out but not separated out altogether; the relations between this limited number of figures and a persistent collective figure then becoming the dominant concerns of the form.

These relations changed perception (articulation) of the collective and of the separated figures, and decisively – for the acted and interacting form was now dynamic – were means of exploring, acting out, these given and possible identifying forms. It would be very much simpler if we could say that the chorus, as a collective mode, was a norm by which the separated figures were judged, yet of course this was not so; the chorus, though usually powerful, was often ignorant or proved to be wrong. It would also be simpler if we could say that the separated figures were all that mattered, yet though they claimed major attention they remained enclosed, by the form, within the choral presence. What we actually find, in the form as a whole, and taking account of its many variations and internal developments, is this culturally specific articulation of dynamic relations between the unique and the common, the singular and the collective, and this articulation intersects with other forms of discourse and with the practical history of a society under major transitional pressures.

The form was also characterized by a specific combination of means of production. There were three modes of the voice, in singing, recitative and speaking. Most of the singing was choral (in semi-choruses); one important part was solo with choral. Simple forms of instrumental music and of dance were integrated with the choral singing and, in the case of music, with the recitative. Conventional forms of movement were integrated with recitative and speech, in three types – indications, motions and postures. There was a limited use of painted scene, and of costumes and masks. It is clear that this dramatic form and practice must then be classified in a broader way, culturally, than is possible in most subsequent dramatic forms and practices. What came later to be predominantly selected as definitively 'dramatic' was only one part of this form – acted dialogue between individuals – and only one of its means of production – acted speech, though the use of 'scene' (spectacle) was also very generally expanded.

Opera and neo-classical drama

As it happens we have two major cases of relatively conscious 'revival' of the classical Greek form, in later periods and in different social orders. They show radically different selections from the range of this form. The first, Italian opera, from c.1600, selected choral and solo singing and recitative. The second, French mid-seventeenth-century neo-classical tragedy, selected formal speech. In the latter case, where a number of plays were based on the same stories as the Greek tragedies, the social content of the formal changes is especially clear. For what had been dropped was not only the singing but the socio-formal element to which it primarily related, the chorus. That collective element of the form was displaced by an extension of inter-personal relations; the limited number of individual figures was decisively extended. Some, but only some, of the dramatic functions of the chorus were replaced by the new formal element of prince and confidential servant. This acted relation carried argument and general clarification, as in some Greek chorus-actor exchanges. But it did not carry the dynamic interrelations of separated figures and an actively present collective, for that social dimension had gone. On the other hand it carried new elements: the confession of private (confidential) feelings, within the problematic relation between private actuality and public possibility; and conscious intrigue, within the stressed political character of a courtly and aristocratic society.

Thus though the prince is continuous, as a figure, his relations with a dramatizable metaphysical order (as in the often acted Greek gods) and with a continually dramatized collective (the chorus) have been replaced by an at once narrower and more deliberately explored set of personal and political relations, to which the new formal conventions correspond. Conflict then normally occurs within this range of relations, and is articulated in a spoken dialogue of uniform verse, by contrast with the many dramatized levels of relationship and the diversity of metre and mode of the earlier form. The major pressures towards this kind of social articulation can also be estimated by the contrast with the other 'inheritor' of the Greek form, Italian opera, where the relative abandonment of this speech-relation element permitted an extraordinarily rich development of music and spectacle. What then happened was a cultural specialization, of different modes and centres of interest, to a point where it became customary to see opera and drama as not only different forms but different arts.

English Renaissance drama

Meanwhile, within the different social order of Renaissance England, quite other formal innovations were made. The 'dramatic', by the late sixteenth century, was a highly specific combination of acted dialogue between individuals and developed spectacle. Making its way in popular rather than primarily aristocratic theatres, it drew heavily on those arts of visual representation (in both acting and scene) which had been central in a popular pre-literate culture. Acts of violence, for example, were now directly staged, rather than narrated or reported. Drama as visible action, without words, was available in the simple form of the dumb-show or in the highly developed forms of staged processions, battles or visions. (In a later, more socially exclusive period, this element developed into a predominant or even separate form, as in the masque, which at an earlier stage had been one of the dramatic sources). Music and song were also used, but with rare exceptions not integrally but as isolated elements of performance.

Then within this synthesis of elements of a popular processional and pageant-based drama, and influenced by but going beyond the terms of a more articulate religious-didactic and humanist form of dialogue, a new kind of dramatic speech emerged, as a profoundly innovative and at least in some major examples temporarily dominant element. And then what is most remarkable, sociologically, about this form of dramatic speech is its deliberate diversity.

It was, first, linguistically co-extensive with the whole range of its society. It included, in one part of its range, highly abstract or formal argument, in the vocabulary of the highly educated, as well as elements of formal verse, in received and closely structured forms. But it included also, in diverse as well as some regular relations with these, the everyday language and speech-forms of war, politics, business and trades, as well as the wide vocabulary and speech-forms (including the 'vulgar' speech-forms) of everyday popular discourse. This socio-linguistic range is still exceptional in drama, and it relates, undoubtedly, to a highly specific (in fact relatively brief) social situation.

But then it was also, in the action, formally co-extensive with an exceptional diversity of types of relationship, over a range from the most formally public to the publicly active, through intrigue and counter-intrigue, to the directly familial and the intimately private, and, beyond these again, to quite new forms of 'inner' speech – the direct composition not only of forms of intellectual and emotional process but also, and significantly, of these processes in radical confusion and breakdown. The relations of each of these ranges to the persistently important forms of visual representation were dynamic and again diverse; at times remarkably integrated; at times, and indeed eventually, unstable.

It is then indeed not easy to speak of a single form; various classifications of types of form are in practice necessary. Yet at a deeper level, and especially in any historical comparison, there was an undoubted *community of forms*, which was both socially specific and again (as in the case of classical Greek tragedy) unrepeatable even where consciously imitated.

The specificity of this community of forms is most evident when it is compared with its English successors. For there is a direct correspondence between the increasing social exclusiveness of the theatres (beginning as early as 1610, with the general move to the indoor 'private' theatres as predominant, continuing to the Civil War and then at its most acute and formally legislated in the period of the Restoration) and what is at once a linguistic and formal shrinkage and a new linguistic and formal regularization. This is one of those important cases in which correspondence between the conditions of a practice and its dominant forms is relatively direct. It is not only what happened in the change from public tragedy to heroic drama. It is also what happened in one of the traceable continuities, in which the often vigorous colloquialism of the post-Restoration comedy of manners (in its other formal functions running back to the earlier class comedies of Fletcher and of Shirley) becomes functionally displaced and isolated: displaced in its limitation to a single and fashionable class; isolated, as a mode, not only from a widely active speech range, but from those more formal modes of language which were crucial elements of the Elizabethan openness.

Changes in the form

Yet the socio-formal changes were in fact much deeper. Elizabethan and especially Shakespearean tragedy admitted, as its shaping form, a quite extraordinarily open interaction of social order and social disintegration. To put it another way, what we can now analyze as 'interaction' found its form in an open and diverse action, within which the forces and terms of order were continuously and actively present, but within which also, and never merely to be disposed of or contained by the forces and terms of order, active forces of disintegration and even dissolution were very powerfully presented, to the point where questions about the nature of the human order itself were directly enacted. Again this form can be more readily recognized by contrast with one of its simpler successors. In Jacobean tragedy this 'integration' has gone. The forces and terms of order have lost substance and have become the forces and terms of power. There are then not only the contending forces of disintegration and dissolution, but the extraordinary dramatization of dissolution in process – the 'war of all against all'.

What was most remarkable about the earlier form – the central major form of the English Renaissance – was its dramatic integration of what could later be separated as 'public' and 'private' questions. The crisis of *Hamlet* or of *King Lear* is a simultaneous crisis of public and private breakdown: not only thematically, but at a deep formal level in the language. In the 'mad' scenes in *Hamlet* and most remarkably in the storm scenes in *King Lear* this reaches through the general actions and questions to what is at once the virtual dissolution of communication –

conventional meanings, sequences and connections radically disturbed and even breaking under the enormous
pressures – and yet, remarkably, the extension of dramatic
language to enact even this process: the total crisis still
enacted, formed. It was in the memory of order, in the
continued desire and evident need for order, in the
contradictions between order and power, and in the deeper
contradictions between a received order or a corrupt power
and the now intensely experienced forces of individual
personality and of a more general mobility: in all these
elements of a total crisis that this remarkable form took
shape. In the later form, which had many continuities with
it, the positive public dimension had gone and a still total
crisis was steadily privatized. Dissolution and horror
became even more emphatic (though not more terrifying)
because they were now contending not with ordering forces
and impulses but, in the end even mechanically, with
themselves.

The forms and history

There are ways of analyzing these changes in terms of the
general history of the society. It is certainly no surprise, in
retrospect, to find a form of total crisis in a society within
forty years of a civil war. It is certainly relevant that the
Jacobean form enacted the condition of the 'war of all
against all' which, in the next generation, was to be taken by
Hobbes as the starting point for a new political philosophy
which 'answered' the dramatically unanswered questions,
in its justification of an absolute safeguarding power. But
the dramatic forms were not anticipations or reflections of
these more general social processes; or rather they are not
to be reduced to anticipations or reflections. For it was in
the deep formal qualities of the dramatic mode itself, and in
the specific qualities of these forms, that the real social
relations were specifically disclosed.

Thus the 'total crisis' is a different matter in dramatic form and in social action, for much the same reasons that the 'war of all against all' is a different matter in dramatic form and in political philosophy. That there are common roots for these different practices is the first (but often only) sociological point. To insist that the practices are different is not some form of reservation, marking off an 'aesthetic' sphere, but a social indication of the actual modes and functions of different practices.

Thus that these evidently related dramatic forms occurred well *before* the forms of political action and the new political philosophy is a point of absolute significance, which must not be lost by some historical elision or some notion of prophecy. When these 'actions' were enacted, in different kinds of practice, they were not the same actions; crucial changes and breaks had occurred. We can say that some dramatic forms, and notably these, enacted elements of the pre-conditions of what could nevertheless, beyond the limits of these forms, be politically acted quite differently. It is not only that the dramatic mode, by its essential cultural properties and signals – its intrinsic capacity, most obviously, to mark the definitive end of an action which in other practices may not be ended or capable of being ended – operates, socially, under different conditions. It is also, as in these specific examples, that these properties and conditions – in the broadest sense, these signals – shape conclusions which are both histori-cally and formally different from those of other practices.

Thus that crucial element of the virtual dissolution of communication which was formally enacted in the crises of Shakespearean tragedy has to be contrasted with the remarkable and extended articulacy with which the Civil War was prepared and fought. And this is not only (though it is crucially) the mark of a different historical period. It is also evidence that the form of the total crisis is different, and that we can only understand what we may still see as related phases of a general crisis if we include all the elements of each practice, those which are discontinuous as well as those which both in analysis and in practice connect.

Moreover the discontinuities have social significance. The crisis of language, and its temporary resolutions, was a central element of the social process of the later seventeenth century. Again, in a more obvious case, the continuities between the Jacobean dramatic form and the Hobbesian ideological assumption have to be set alongside the discontinuity or break: that within the dramatic form absolute power, to stop the chain of killings, did not arrive and was not envisaged, its probable bearers being seen as the next phase of the *same* action rather than its political resolution. The difference is historical and political; it is also formal: for the obvious reason that within a play this kind of catastrophe cannot only seem but be final.

Restoration forms

Yet it is not only a question of catastrophe. One of the effects of the rationalization of absolute power, in a period which was reflecting not so much on internecine dramatic conflicts but upon an actual and bloody civil war, was a form of restoration which, since it only temporarily repressed the underlying conflicts, could achieve little more, as modes, than the abstract or the cynical.

Heroic drama

Thus the heroic drama (e.g., Dryden's *Conquest of Granada*) could abstract and isolate the *attitudes* of a sovereign moral order, but typically not this order in its full (social and political) range of contending forces. What it showed was rather the at once internalized and projected conflict of individual ambitions, desires and restraints, as typically in the conflict between 'love' and 'duty'. This no longer, as in the full substance of *Hamlet* or *King Lear*, convulsed men and women and a kingdom, but ran its course within the bounds of a single figure. The deep conflicts of the new individualism itself, as well as, more obviously, the range of contending social forces now temporarily repressed by the willed notion of absolute sovereignty, were thus radically displaced and excluded.

The comedy of manners

Yet this displacement, at the most sensitive and indeed dangerous level, was accompanied by an extraordinary admission of new social relations, in a specifically dramatizable form. In the comedy of manners (e.g., Wycherley's *The Plain Dealer*) in spite of and in part because of the class limitation already noted, we can recognize an unmistakably bourgeois world, in which money and property, rather than political power of any of the older kinds, were the real as distinct from the attitudinized social preoccupations. Sociologically this is an almost unique dramatic form, in that the congruity between its deliberately limited class audience, its 'gentleman dramatists' drawn from the same limited milieu, and its dramatic material strictly limited to this same *contemporary* life (in itself a major new factor), is quite extraordinarily complete. Brief as it was, in this inevitably temporary congruity, the form at once mediated and composed a set of specific social relations. The preoccupation with money and property, within a highly competitive, self-displaying and intrinsically mobile social order (at this particular class level), was shown to be inextricable from the real and feigned loves and appetites of a system of propertied marriage, in the particular milieu of the London 'season', where the contacts were meant to be made and the bargains struck, and where there were necessarily also the attendants and the exploiters of this general class process.

Seen, almost exclusively, from this precise and limited point of vantage, the process materialized as a form with specific (tied) characteristics, but also, interestingly, with innovative elements which would outlast its close context.

Thus the candour (often the coarse candour) of its recognition and imitation of the manners and motives of its world is at one level inextricable from the active cynicism (which is then sometimes more than cynicism) of people who understand the process too well – and understand it both as reality and as game – to pretend that things are otherwise. Of course, from any other social position, both the process and these attitudes towards it were morally objectionable; some such protests have continued to our own day. Yet what can be isolated as a locally explicable (and ambiguous) candour has also, historically, to be seen as a moment of a much more general transition. The generalization of a quasi-colloquial form of dramatic speech (quasi-colloquial, as all such modes must be, yet here especially so, since there is a direct congruity between forms of theatrical and social artifice) was now sufficiently advanced (though not yet complete, as the retention of rhymed prologues and epilogues and of 'sentences' – summary moral indications – reminds us) to serve as a mark in one of the major transitions of the new social order which was being entered. Again, but more completely, the shift to contemporary and to indigenous material, as the normal subjects for drama, occurred here in very special conditions but was to become the significant and distinguishing emphasis of the drama of a whole new epoch.

Thus we find the apparent paradox of the appearance of two or three of the major elements of the drama of the bourgeois epoch in the highly specific form of one of the most socially exclusive sites of any drama: a fashionable aristocratic world around a London court. Yet while the heroic drama can be reasonably interpreted as the ideology (and then only the ideology) of a true restoration, the comedy of manners, in its deliberately limited area (and surely with the advantages of just this limitation) has to be seen as a remaking of dramatic form to negotiate the decisively altered relations of a competitive, mobile and bargaining social order, in which title and property were both determined and seen as determined, in ways and by values radically different from those of a feudal and post-feudal, even disintegrating post-feudal world.

It was this 'seeing as differently determined' that shaped the new form, and here the undoubted pressure of some older ways of seeing – that other part of candour which is not merely coarse recognition but a value to be set, however tentatively and self-protectively, against a pervasively devious, calculating and deceiving 'way of the world' – interacted to give the form a strength which its immediate successors, more consciously moral but for a long while as unwilling to see as to accept, conspicuously lacked.

Bourgeois rama

The complexity of this example stands indeed in marked contrast to the immediately succeeding phase. For what emerged in England in the first half of the eighteenth century was an exceptionally simple type of what can be called, in the strictest sense, bourgeois drama. Here, indeed, we find the clearest case, in the whole history of drama, of an ideological consciousness of new social relations being brought to bear on the reconstruction of a form:

> Long has the Fate of Kings and Empires been
> The common business of the Tragic Scene,
> As if Misfortune made the Throne her seat,
> And none could be unhappy but the Great . . .

> Stories like this with Wonder we may hear,
> But far remote, and in a higher Sphere,
> We ne'er can pity what we ne'er can share.

Accordingly,

> Stripp'd of Regal Pomp, and glaring Show
> His Muse reports a tale of Private Woe
> Works up Distress from Common Scenes in Life
> A Treach'rous Brother, and an Injur'd Wife.

This exceptional class consciousness, though leading in the short run to little significant drama (the most interesting example is Lillo's *The London Merchant*) is a clear sign of a new social order. It is also an indirect indication of the way in which a once powerful form could decay from within, until the eventual attack on it was on an empty shell.

Rank in drama

It is of course true that the regular association of almost all serious drama with princes and ruling families had been in part the reflection of social orders in which they were predominant. This was especially the case in Renaissance drama. But in Greek tragedy, for example, the sociological connection had been quite different. This was a drama of ancient ('heroic') ruling families within the quite different contemporary order of the city-state. Its characters and actions were thus not a reflection of existing social relations. For these, as we have seen, we have to look more deeply, at the chorus-and-actors form. Yet the regular association, or even identity, of the fate of a prince or ruling family with the more general fate of a state or a city made possible a form of integrated action in which the individual character, the social position and responsibility, the general wellbeing of the community and the broadest sense of the human situation could be seen in a single if always complex dimension. The prince or ruling family, it can then be said, was an agency of the most general social and metaphysical (indeed, strictly, socio-metaphysical) concerns.

But already in Imperial Rome such actions had to some extent narrowed, and the fate of princes, as such, was given a prominence, as a definition of serious drama, which persisted to the Renaissance and beyond. In English Renaissance drama, as we have seen, there were many important cases in which the fate of the prince and the fate of his kingdom were radically connected, at many levels from the obvious connection with good or bad government (as in Shakespeare's English history and Roman plays) to the deeper and more extended connections of the major tragedies, where *Hamlet* without the state of Denmark, *King Lear* without the state of Britain, *Macbeth* without the state of Scotland, and through each of these states a more general human condition, would lose most of their significance.

At the same time, however, and even (and not always in complex ways) in these major plays, an ordering of relative significance by social rank had also penetrated deeply into the form. Characters from the lower or intermediate classes were often given a different dramatic status from the beginning: as agents of comic relief; as the colloquial (prose) English in a British or foreign court; as objects in dialogue, where what mattered was what the prince said to or drew from them. It is then the intrinsic confusion between these two functions of rank in drama – the convincing reflection or imagination of a general condition which can be concentrated or exemplified in a prince and his state; on the other hand the assumption of an autonomous connection between rank and human significance – which needs, even today, to be resolved.

What the eighteenth-century bourgeois ideologists saw and attacked was the second function. In missing the first, they had, for some time, the paradoxical effect of making the drama less public, of attempting to confine it (in the new separated terms) to 'private woe'. The later major bourgeois drama, from Ibsen, remade, as we shall see, a public drama within these new social relations, but most ordinary bourgeois drama has continued to operate within the terms of this reduction; ('drama is about people, not about public questions', as if the *Oresteia, King Lear* and *Rosmersholm* had never been written). On the other hand, the resolute attack on the assumptions of the second function, the insistence that any life, whatever its social rank, required serious attention –

> From lower life we draw our Scene's Distress;
> – Let not your Equals move your Pity less

– was necessary not only as an inauguration of that fully extended and fully inclusive drama, in modern social terms, which has since been predominant, but as a way of getting rid of the decadent forms in which, because of changes in the social order, the general substance had withered or vanished, and all that was left was the 'pomp', the 'glaring Show' or the rhetoric of rank.

Factors of Bourgeois drama

By the mid-eighteenth century, if still in early and relatively crude ways, the determining factors of almost all modern dramatic forms had in fact made their appearance. In bourgeois tragedy, as in the comedy of manners, the material of drama was coming, if still hesitantly, to be defined as *contemporary* (by contrast with almost all previous drama) and, in association with this, *indigenous*, in the sense that there could now be a normal expectation of congruity, when desired, between the time, place and milieu of the dramatic action and of the dramatic performance. (There were of course still hesitations, as in the notable case of Lillo's *The London Merchant*, where a wholly indigenous and in spirit contemporary action is hedged by a reference back to the late sixteenth century.) A third factor, the generalization of a quasi-colloquial form of dramatic speech, was already present in the comedy of manners though its full development in bourgeois tragedy was to come through much later. It was not a norm – certainly not the powerful and directive norm it later became – until the nineteenth century. The fourth and fifth factors are the most direct contributions of bourgeois tragedy: the new social extension and inclusiveness, so that all lives, regardless of rank, could become the material of serious drama, and (though with residual ambiguities) a new secularism, itself confirming tendencies already evident in the Renaissance. This secularism is not so much a matter of attitudes to religious belief, or of opinion or reference, as a process of steadily excluding from the dramatic action any supernatural intervention or agency, so that the human action, however judged, is played in exclusively human terms. These five factors, taken together, have provided the basis for the distinctive deep signals and conventions of modern drama.

Developments in bourgeois drama

Yet we must also see that the drama of the last two hundred and fifty years has gone through its own evolution of specific forms, on this general basis and with some significant variations of emphasis between the distinctive factors. We can now trace some main lines of this evolution in selected major examples, showing the effects of changes in actual social relations and in their formal articulation.

Naturalism

The key case is that of *naturalism*. This can be seen as either the whole point of view, and thus the general deep form established by these five factors, or, alternatively, one general form which realized these tendencies in a specifically ordered way. There is something to be said for both interpretations, but both must be distinguished from a very weak if common sense of naturalism, in which one of the factors – the generalization of a quasi-colloquial form of dramatic speech – is taken as definitive, often flanked by a version of the fifth factor – secularism – in a specialized sense of the limitation of dramatic action to 'probable' human behaviour. In fact, since naturalist practice has been heavily marked also by the other three factors – the contemporary, the indigenous and the socially extended or inclusive – this ordinary sense misdirects the whole argument, making it at once too general – a specific form seems to be the whole movement – and too narrowly technical, in that the selected devices of quasi-colloquial speech and 'probable' behaviour are abstracted from the deeper complex of determining social relationships and perspectives. There is a sense, which we must maintain, in which the whole movement represented by the five factors has to be emphasized as dominant in modern drama as a whole. Indeed in most breaks from and revolts against what is commonly called naturalism, most of these factors continued to be determining. We can then make real distinction only if we look for specific variations, combinations and hierarchies.

Thus the crucial distinguishing quality of naturalism, as a dramatic form, is a specific variation of the fifth factor, secularism, of course in combination with the other four. Where in other modern forms, as we shall see, secularism could be a merely neutral abstention from supernatural interventions or agencies, or even a negative awareness of the loss of such a dimension, in naturalism it was a positive emphasis, which produced a quite specific new form. This emphasis, which led to deep changes in formal conventions, was a matter of quite newly perceived relations between human actions and a material environment. That is to say, the physical world in which men found themselves, but also the material world and the socially materialized world which they encountered and recognized as humanly made, were now inevitable and often decisive elements of any significant dramatic action.

To put the point sharply, the major naturalist dramatists did not prescribe a new kind of dramatic scene, the detailed physical realization of a room or some other physical environment on the then qualitatively altered stage, for *technical* reasons, or because new techniques of stage carpentry and lighting made this more feasible. They put on these rooms, prescribed in detail in a new form of writing which was much more than mere 'stage direction', because such immediate physical environments were, in their view, necessary elements of the dramatic action. They were, in the fullest sense, *living* rooms: places made to live in in certain ways: environments which both reflected and influenced their possibilities of life.

Material locations of drama

At the deepest level this new sense of the material environment, this physical grasp of a man-made world, is profoundly characteristic of the bourgeois and especially the capitalist social order. The altered relations between men and things, which found their fullest expression in the new urban industrial economy, were represented in drama in these new conventions. What in almost all earlier drama had been primarily a playing space, with a few simple signals of immediate location or at most the represented outline of a location, became, in this general movement, first a more fully represented 'real place' and finally, in high naturalism, a tangible presence: the 'stage as room': the room soaking into the lives of the persons as their lives had soaked into it. The classic example of this mode is Ibsen's *The Wild Duck*.

Naturalism and representation

Yet we must then distinguish between authentic naturalism and the more general movement of bourgeois physical representation. There are active and passive forms of the basic convention of a significant relationship between men and their physical environment. In majority bourgeois drama, the convention required appropriate 'settings' of lives, and this was especially necessary in the social extension of dramatic actions. In a more limited social mode the physical representation of a palace or a castle could indeed be ancillary – generally indicative – but now the precise settings of much more varied kinds of life were necessary parts of their realization. Yet this could be relatively passive: the 'sort of place' in which 'such people' would live; at its edges, even – as still commonly – a mere display of place, indicating but not otherwise defining.

It is confusing that this has been so generally called 'naturalism'. For authentic naturalism was always a critical movement, in which the relations between men and their environments were not merely represented but actively explored. Indeed, though in its period it is quite evidently a bourgeois form, it is also, on its record, part of the critical and self-critical wing of the bourgeoisie. In Ibsen and Zola, early Strindberg and Chekhov, O'Casey and O'Neill, it accepted the deep convention of significant (and by the new methods dramatizable) relations between men and their living or working environments, but commonly as the literal staging of the radical questions: how do we, how can we, how should we live in this specifically tangible place and way of life?

This was the decisive reintroduction of a public dimension into a privatized mode. It was of course a bourgeois reintroduction, since the site of decisive action, understandably no longer the palace, was the private family room: a room, however, that was predominantly shown as a trap: the centre of significant immediate relationships, but with larger determining forces operating beyond it, to be looked at from the window or to arrive as messages which would reshape these lives. The form thus expressed a precise contradiction in bourgeois social relationships: that the centre of values was the individual and the family, but that the mode of production which sustained them – the world they went out into and returned from – was in a quite different social range, much wider, more complex and more arbitrary. And significantly, within this form, this wider world could not be directly dramatized, as in the older and simpler actions of kings, although at this level of seriousness it was known to be determining.

Tensions of the bourgeois form

It was from the tensions of this profound contradiction that the new forms of twentieth-century drama were created Before the 1890s the naturalists were the only significant fraction within a generally bourgeois dramatic world The minority 'free theatres' which were spreading through Europe at that time were mainly under their influence. They represented the most positive, fact-facing and consciously enlightened sector of the class: at one level liberal and reforming; at another level, within the contradiction, profoundly uneasy about bourgeois civilization itself, though as yet with no alternatives to it. But then from the 1890s a sense of total crisis developed very rapidly, and as in the somewhat comparable crisis of the late sixteenth and early seventeenth centuries there was a remarkable efflorescence both of drama generally and of new forms.

Breaks to new forms

This is an exceptionally complex process to analyse, whether sociologically or formally. But we can make a preliminary working distinction of three kinds of form, each increasingly sustained by a distinctive ideology, which can be seen (of course with some confusion and overlapping) as corresponding to three discernible formations within the crisis of late bourgeois society. It is characteristic of this new period that it was marked (as in the closely comparable case of painting) by a profusion of named movements, many of them, following naturalism, conscious enough to be 'isms'.

In any full analysis we would have to trace each of these often short-lived movements, but on the other hand to analyze the history from the temporary labels would be to miss the significance of the deeper and broader alternative directions and forms. Thus, though many kinds of variation would have to be added, we can best begin a social analysis of twentieth-century dramatic forms by distinguishing three main kinds, which we can provisionally call *subjective expressionism, social expressionism* and *symbolic abstraction*. In a full history, in addition of course to the persistence of older forms (which still occupied the majority of theatres), we would have also to add the development of naturalism under consciously socialist influences.

Symbolic abstraction

Subjective expressionism and social expressionism were both breaks beyond naturalism. Symbolic abstraction, by contrast, was an attempted break back. Associated almost everywhere with explicit political and cultural reaction, it sought to cancel not only the naturalist but the most general bourgeois emphases. What it sought, dramatically, was an effective restoration of a metaphysical dimension: at times, as in some of the work of T. S. Eliot, by inserting explicitly religious elements; more widely by the conscious revival of 'myth' and 'legend' in their modern senses, as the metaphysical substitutes for religion in a predominantly secular world (cf. the plays of W. B. Yeats). Very widely, however, in work of this kind, the modes of an older drama were used, of course selectively, as a form of revival: mask, chorus, certain kinds of verse; plots and characters from the old plays (or from these and the 'myths'). By these devices, this movement sought to go back beyond the bourgeois ('commercial' and 'materialist') world, but even more specifically to provide alternatives to the frankly social world which bourgeois drama had emphasized, and to the values of democracy and rationality which had followed from it. These were then political and cultural alternatives, effected as dramatic forms: specifically the alternatives of the mysterious, the inexplicable and the ungraspable.

In different examples this movement rejected each of the five factors of bourgeois drama; in the most evident cases, all five together. But there was then a complex overlap with an area that was being differently developed by subjective expressionism: the new symbolism of an effectively hidden and mysterious area which was not, like that of earlier orders, beyond man in some supernatural dimension, but within him, in the 'unconscious'. It is necessary here to make a sharp distinction between those formulations of 'the unconscious' which are in the spirit of analysis and explication (as in the original impetus of Freud) – modes which are indeed often compatible with naturalism – and those other formulations in which 'unconscious forces' function as a modern metaphysics: the inexplicable forces which at a level 'much deeper than society' determine human lives, and are graspable only as symbols, in dramatic or some other artistic form.

Thus, though the movement was explicitly anti-bourgeois, in both a general and a formal sense, it was also, at a deeper level, the culmination of the weakest tendency of the bourgeois epoch: the attempted stabilization, at a new level of abstraction from society and from history, of the mystery of general human processes: a mystery now finally located – for this is its bourgeois character, as distinct from earlier metaphysical forms – within the *individual*.

Subjective expressionism

Subjective expressionism, by contrast, though it shared this emphasis on the 'unconscious', and even further isolated the 'individual', worked in a quite opposite direction from stabilization, and was then not concerned with a restoration of 'dramatic order' supported by the adaptation of ritual elements to theatrical forms. The main and highly original impulse of subjective expressionism was the dramatization of isolation and exposure: the cry of the lost individual in a meaningless world. Originating, as it did, within the tensions of late high naturalism, it steadily excluded all those elements of the dramatic form which could be seen as merely contingent to this crisis. The solidly grasped physical world of the naturalist play was dissolved into the (consciously and necessarily) distorted images of its isolated, agonized perception. The steadily formulated social group of both naturalist and pre-naturalist drama was transformed into dramatic characters who were primarily functions of a single isolated consciousness, whether that of a central character, like the Stranger in Strindberg's *To Damascus*, or, in later developments, that of the dramatist himself, whose play is the projection of his deliberately isolated world, as in late Beckett.

Thus both the given material environment and the given social relationships were radically excluded from the form, so as to emphasize, first, the isolated individual and his projected world, but then, second, a reduction beyond even this, to broken fragments of individuals who can barely even recognize their own projections. It can be said that this is a bourgeois form, in its passage from the isolation of the individual to the loss of even that individuality. But sociologically it is crucial to emphasize that in all its stages it has been radically detached from the bourgeoisie *as a class in society*. It is formally and experientially detached, since it has ceased all dealings with a shared social and human world, yet on the other hand, and of course inevitably, it is still practically attached to a social process, within which its forms are produced and shared.

At its strongest this unwilling and ambiguous attachment is to the victims of the dominant order, to all those who have experienced meaninglessness and breakdown. This is the deep source of its power. But the form has this further paradox. In late Chekhov, at the crisis of high naturalism, the social group which could grasp its own world was already dissolving. Indeed the originality of Chekhov was that he found new kinds of action and language to express just such a dissolution: a shared breakdown and loss of meaning. His determining form is then that of the *negative group*. The people are all still there, and trying to communicate, but have actually lost touch with each other and with their world: a loss realized in their dramatic language, which is that of people speaking at or past rather than to or with each other.

That is one kind of generalization of the loss of meaning and contact. It has been widely imitated, in what is called the 'drama of non-communication'. But in subjective expressionism even the minimal figures of the negative group have gone. The individual is radically isolated and is unable, *a priori*, to grasp his world. Thus what may begin as a specific condition – this individual is a stranger to himself and to others – is presented dramatically as a general condition. It is then received at many levels, over a range from serious recognition of the conditions of alienation – a phenomenon which can then, but not within this form, be socially and culturally analyzed – to what is really, and quite commonly, the regular and even enjoyable consumption of dramatically alienated others. It is significant that in its later phases the tragic and agonized spirit of the early experiments has become predominantly comic and even consciously entertaining. To understand this fully, the form has to be analysed not only in itself but in its actual productive institutions.

The form pulled both ways. The fundamental tension of high naturalism can be defined as its intense awareness of powerful and relatively unseen forces which were pulling the form – and within the form every kind of observation and interpretation – in apparently opposite directions. On the one hand there was an awareness of the processes of the deepest kinds of individual consciousness. The dramatic speech of high naturalism, in Ibsen, early Strindberg or Chekhov, is never limited to flat representation of probable conversation, but uses many devices to reveal, indicate or at least suggest the inner pressures which limit or influence or distort what can, in this mode, be said. At the same time, there was an at least equal awareness of the most general social processes – historical moments, the condition of a particular people, economic pressures, the condition of the family and of marriage, the general complex of institutions and beliefs.

What high naturalism selected as its form was a kind of middle ground where all these extended processes could be shown as interacting, on the chosen site of the domestic group and its immediate relationships. Yet what was shown was never a neutral interaction, but in a number of ways the crisis of such interaction: a crisis which was often most evident in the very failure to articulate (in their own terms but also in relating and interacting terms) the full processes which lay beyond the 'middle ground' of the form. It was not a blank failure; indeed the struggle to hold and extend this ground was heroic.

But in the period of total crisis from the 1890s the hold began to fail, and there was a fracture of forms which was also, to some degree, a fracture of institutions and audiences. We have already seen how subjective expressionism, in the many forms indicated by that general description, was a move away from the middle ground, and thus from the temporarily stabilized naturalist form, towards the often hidden processes of individual consciousness. Its forms were built, we can now see, from states which could be held to reveal these processes, in sufficiently manifest shapes: dreams, nightmares, breakdowns, conditions of extreme exposure (the formal development, in this sense, from Strindberg's *Dreamplay* to Beckett's *Endgame*, is clear).

Social expressionism

The apparently opposite move, towards social expressionism, shared some of the same formal elements. The deeper and relatively hidden forces of historical and social movements were to be revealed at moments of extreme crisis: wars, revolutions, strikes and other forms of social struggle. The major period of this work runs from Toller and Kaiser in the 1920s, through the epic theatre of Brecht to much of the radical drama of our own time. Such work overlapped and shared an audience with the only serious continuation of high naturalism, in those various forms of social realism in which there was an attempt to re-establish the 'middle ground' on the site not of the domestic but of the social or class group. Social expressionism typically projected and polarized the contending social forces, while social realism typically described and 'represented' them. But in either case there was a search for new audiences, beyond the progressive fractions which had sustained the earlier new theatres. Typically the new social forms sought a new class audience, though they by no means always found it.

The social relations of such forms – internally, in their definitions of the sites on which reality was critically generated; externally, in their proposed relations with those who would assent to or learn from these – were thus radically different from those of the bourgeois drama, though most still necessarily operated within the general conditions of a bourgeois society. Symbolic abstraction, in quite different ways, was seeking its own consciously minority audiences; its physically and ideologically 'little' theatres. The main body of bourgeois theatre continued with its received forms: often the cultivation of an increasingly barren middle ground; more often the exploitation of the isolated theatrical elements of action and display. Characteristically it also incorporated, at a relatively later stage, some of the successful examples of the dissident forms. Its most successful incorporation was in that of some of the more negotiable forms of subjective expressionism, which in its diluted emphasis on 'psycho-logical conditions' and on the distortions of subjectivity was nearer its own preoccupations.

The analysis of the altered social relations of drama is more general. The insoluble crisis of the central and still dominant received form led to an extraordinarily rich proliferation of alternative forms but also to quite new conditions of fragmentation. What happened in the theatre was repeated, on a vastly expanded scale, in the cinema and television, which became the new major dramatic institutions. Intensely productive and vigorous, the institutions are by comparison with any earlier period profoundly eclectic, and within this eclecticism, in some quite new ways, some actual social struggles are being fought out in the competition between alternative dramatic forms.

This is the sociological and formal basis for the necessary contrast with the earlier situations which we have analysed. There we could see, in historically phased examples, major connections between forms of social relations and specific dramatic forms. Such connections can be traced, in the same historical perspective, in other artistic forms. Drama has advantages in such analysis, because of its very long historical record, but there have been important comparable analyses of painting (Hauser, 1962; Klingender, 1972), of music (Adorno, 1949), of the novel (Lukács, 1962; Goldmann, 1964) and of poetry (Benjamin, 1969).

Methodologically, we can make a distinction, within the general assumptions of such analysis, between degrees of relative emphasis on formal and historical elements, where both are still taken as linked. Indeed it is in just this area that there are still central controversies of principle and of method. Yet without reducing the relevance of these theoretical controversies, it can be observed that there is a certain necessary shift, in analyses of modern cultural production, towards comparative formal analysis, since it is a general fact of modern cultures that alternative or apparently alternative forms are produced within the complexities as well as the conflicts of modern extended societies, by comparison or by contrast with the dominance or even monopoly of a single form in earlier social situations.

This cannot mean (as it has sometimes been taken) that we should move from historical-formal to purely formal theory and analysis. On the contrary, the historical basis of all socio-formal analysis should be seen as reinforced by the historical character of this shift from singular to multiple forms of cultural composition. The case of drama, with its full range of historical and formal evidence, is then especially important as an indication of these connected principles.

7 Reproduction

Most actual sociology of culture has been relatively successful when it has been concerned with specific forms, practices, institutions or periods, and relatively unsuccessful when it has attempted either to generalize these as social processes or to develop a general theory within which they might (all) be understood. There seem to be two main reasons for this difference of result.

The first is a matter of specificity and complexity. It seems undeniable that the more we know of a particular form, practice, institution or period the less likely we are to be satisfied with any general analysis of it, however close. This dissatisfaction is healthy when it leads to grounded objections, reasoned amendments and, above all, further detailed investigation. Yet we ought not to overlook the specific cultural components of a kind of dissatisfaction which often sounds much like this, with the constructive moves reiterated as desirable but not actually made, or with such moves reduced to what can properly be called particularism. For there is a kind of attachment to specificity and complexity which is the condition of any adequate intellectual work, and another kind which is really a defence of a particular kind of consciousness, within very specific cultural conditions: a defence, really, against recognition of the necessarily general relations within which all cultural work, including analysis, is done.

Such defences are easily and even habitually sustained within certain kinds of privileged institution, where privilege is not so much, or not primarily, a matter of income or life style, but rather a condition of relatively distanced, relatively unchallenged relations with the practical and continuing social process.

Thus we have always to distinguish between two kinds of consciousness: that alert, open and usually troubled recognition of specificity and complexity, which is always, in a thousand instances, putting working generalizations and hypotheses under strain; and that other, often banal, satisfaction with specificity and complexity, as reasons for the endless postponement of all (even local) general judgements or decisions. Difficult as it often is to distinguish between these modes, in any isolated moment, the significance of the distinction has to be strongly emphasized: not only because it is critical in the development of conditions for more general work, but also because it is a relevant instance of a process with which we must now closely concern ourselves: that of *cultural reproduction*.

In societies like our own there can be an effective kind of cultural reproduction within the very processes of knowledge. An educational system can promote rigorous training in reliable procedures of knowledge and analysis, so that many of us can then know and analyze. Or (as I think now commonly) it can be directed to induce an endlessly knowledgeable helplessness, in the sheer scale of what is to be known and its virtually infinite exceptions. And then at this level (but only at this level, for at some prescribed leaving age we are expected to go on and take up positions in the world) nothing is certain enough to be reliable, and there is only the (highly specific and complex) inertia of the (relatively unknowable) 'way of the world'.

The second reason for the difference of success between

specific and more general studies (well beyond this first area in which 'success' itself is, for the reasons mentioned, a local and variable cultural criterion) can be found in the character of the types of generalization and theory which have been most commonly attempted. These have been discussed at various points in the previous chapters, but their two most common features can be summarized. There is, first, their supra- or extra-historical character – so that reasonable or demonstrable generalizations for a given period or epoch are assumed to be capable of universal application. Then, second, there is the relative predominance of a certain kind of philosophy over the available methods of sociology, so that the very concepts which need to be constructed by historical and sociological analysis are assumed, often in received forms, either as the necessary grounds of theoretical proof or at best as the framework for any investigation which has intentions beyond the most scattered empiricism. The difficulty then is that all analytic construction has to begin from some (and in practice some of these) concepts, and yet that they can so easily come to direct all stages of the inquiry, or, as has happened recently, in general cultural theory, to absorb research into their own forms. And this, we can note, is a further instance, at the most theoretical but often determining levels, of cultural reproduction.

In practice, and with an effort of will, we can select from the available concepts, by criteria drawn from observation of the relative successes and failures of previous kinds of inquiry. And here 'cultural reproduction' is especially interesting. It is first, necessarily, a temporal concept, involving movement from one dateable manifestation of culture to another, though, as we shall see, this does not mean that it is always historical. Second, it is, except in its most abstract and dogmatic forms, a negotiable concept, in that at least in its working propositions it is brought into early contact with hard evidence. Third, and most significantly, it has an initial general appropriateness to certain observed qualities of cultural process. There are, we shall see, many problems of precise definition, and of necessary distinctions. But it can be said in general that it is inherent in the concept of a culture that it is capable of being reproduced; and, further, that in many of its features culture is indeed a mode of reproduction.

Reproducibility

What is true of 'a culture', at its most general level – that it is never a form in which people happen to be living, at some isolated moment, but a selection and organization, of past and present, necessarily providing for its own kinds of continuity – is true also, at different levels, of many of the elements of cultural process. Thus a form is inherently reproducible; that is its necessary definition as form Signals and conventions are inherently reproductive, or they lose their significance. Language as such, or any language or system of non-verbal communication, exists only to the degree that it is capable of reproduction. A tradition is the process of reproduction in action. Thus many of the key elements of cultural process are brought together by this concept. But then it is also apparent, even in these early definitions, that 'reproduction' itself has different levels of meaning and bearing. Indeed, if it is too simply and hastily used, it can overlay rather than clarify the actual processes.

Meanings of 'reproduction'

There is, first, an obvious problem in the word. Since the nineteenth century, 'reproduction' has had the common meaning of a copy, or making a copy. This is familiar, for example, in the 'reproductions' of (original) paintings, and the sense was used, in Chapter 4 above, to describe processes of mechanical or electronic copying. Meanwhile, of course, in biology, including human biology, 'reproduction' has the common meaning of making a new organism within the same species, but here crucially not as a copy. In ordinary usage we can distinguish these meanings, and further distinguish between the contrasting processes: mechanical or electronic copying, where the criterion of the process is the making of accurate copies – reproduction in a *uniform* sense; on the other hand biological generation, where typically forms – species – are prolonged, but in intrinsically variable individual examples – reproduction in a *genetic* sense.

It is then of great importance, when the word is taken across to describe cultural processes, not only to be aware of these radical differences of meaning and bearing, but to avoid any premature decision on which of the two senses is appropriate to cultural applications. Indeed, since the applications are at all early stages metaphorical (and with metaphors drawn from such contrasting processes), there can in any case be no simple transfer. There are very few significant cultural processes analogous to the printing press or the photocopier, but there are also very few analogous to sexual or other biological reproduction, with their precisely knowable physical elements and combinations of elements. These are the complexities of the concept, but we can still usefully retain some of its general indications, thinking with it rather than under it.

Education

Thus some concept of reproduction is necessary if we are to have any critical sociology of, for example, either education or tradition. It is characteristic of educational systems to claim that they are transmitting 'knowledge' or 'culture' in an absolute, universally derived sense, though it is obvious that different systems, at different times and in different countries, transmit radically different selective versions of both. Moreover it is clear, as Bourdieu (1977) and others have shown, that there are fundamental and necessary relations between this selective version and the existing dominant social relations. These can be seen in the disposition of a curriculum, in the modes of selection of those who are to be educated and in what ways, and in definitions of educational (pedagogic) authority. It is then reasonable, at one level, to speak of the general educational process as a key form of cultural reproduction, which can be linked with that more general reproduction of existing social relations which is assured by existing and self-prolonging property and other economic relations, institutions of state and other political power, religious and family forms. To ignore these links is to submit to the arbitrary authority of a self-proclaimed 'autonomous' system.

But there are then two problems. that there may, in these linked processes, be significant kinds of unevenness and asymmetry, or in other words different degrees of relative autonomy; and that it is also an observable fact of educational systems, especially in certain periods and societies, that they change both internally and in their general relations with other systems. The metaphor of 'reproduction', if pushed too hard, can obscure these crucial processes of relative autonomy and of change, even while it usefully insists on a general and intrinsic character.

Tradition

The problem can be more clearly seen in the crucial cultural concept of tradition, which I called, provisionally but advisedly, reproduction in action. For tradition ('our cultural heritage') is self-evidently a process of deliberate continuity, yet any tradition can be shown, by analysis, to be a selection and reselection of those significant received and recovered elements of the past which represent not a necessary but a *desired* continuity. In this it resembles education, which is a comparable selection of desired knowledge and of modes of learning and authority. It is important to emphasize, in each case, that this 'desire' is not abstract but is effectively defined by existing general social relations.

Yet there are then differences, both between education and tradition, and between each and other forms of more direct reproduction. Education, it is true, is a highly effective carrier and organizer of tradition, but there are also other social processes, of a less overtly systematic kind, by which a tradition is shaped and reshaped. Indeed it is characteristic of tradition, and of crucial importance for its place in culture, that under certain social conditions alternative and even antagonistic traditions can be generated within the same society. Much general history, and also the specializing histories of art or literature, are evidently parts of this process, in which alternative examples of admirable or desirable precedents and continuities are practically presented; indeed historiography (and of course theory) provides many examples of this kind of competition or struggle, as well as the more containable but very general cases of amendment and modification of the presented past and its desirable or possible continuities. Such cases range from that operative reselection of the tradition which is necessary to keep it relevant and powerful in changing conditions, to those other cases in which the definition of the process as history requires, by its internal criteria, those kinds of re-examination and re-presentation which are not to be subordinated to the simple demands of cultural reproduction.

Now it is already a necessary amendment of any simple notion of education as cultural reproduction to observe, as we must, that the results of these competing and amending processes – though unevenly, and often with severe local difficulties – make their way into actual education. But there is then this difference from the social operations of tradition, that such entries are commonly subject to institutional negotiation and in the worst cases to institutional control, and thus that they quickly encounter organized and manifest social relations and authorities.

It is not that the workings of alternative traditions present a complete contrast. Access to knowledge and especially to its general distribution is of course socially mediated and in some cases directly controlled. But it is observably easier to present the elements of an alternative or even an oppositional tradition, in the looser and more general relations of a whole cultural process, than it is, for example, to organize an alternative and especially an oppositional educational system. This varies in different periods and societies. The case of asymmetry between a capitalist market and a bourgeois social order, discussed in 2 above, is perhaps especially in our minds, but then it is a very significant and widespread phenomenon. We should also remember that alternative educational systems have at times been successfully instituted, as in the outstanding case of the English nonconformist Dissenting Academies. Yet the general distinction still seems to hold, and what it most usefully indicates, theoretically, is that the degree of relative autonomy of a cultural process is, at a first level, deducible from its practical distance from otherwise organized social relations.

Variable distances of practices

This is then a crucial observation within the definition of cultural reproduction. It is perhaps also a way of distinguishing cultural from more general social reproduction. For we can distinguish, in the whole range of social practice, different and variable measures of distance between particular practices and the social relations which organize them. Thus, in most modern working practices, there is a very close and early – indeed in effect integrated-relation between the possibility of a practice and the conditions of wage-labour, themselves derived from the privileged ownership of the necessary means of production within a capitalist or state-capitalist system. Reproduction of the practice is then in effect inseparable from reproduction of these determining relations, which are at the same time reproduced not only by the continuity of the practice but by the direct and general exertion of economic and political power. It is not that it is impossible to challenge, limit or actually prevent such reproduction; all these actions are possible at the highest levels of industrial and political struggle. But it is a matter of fact that even quite radical amendments of the terms of these relations – as, for example, collective bargaining, increased union powers, or an increased share of the product for its direct producers – are compatible with the still effective reproduction of the deep form of privileged ownership and the consequent general condition of wage-labour. This degree of closeness, this virtual identity, between the conditions of most practices and a deeply organized form of social relations is then the process of reproduction at its most determinate level. (It is also, in practice, the best specification of what is indicated, generally, as 'determination, in the last instance, by the economy.')

But there is then a range of many kinds of practice in which there are actual and variable degrees of distance. Some forms of work, including, as we have seen, some forms of cultural work, operate outside the conditions of wage-labour. Some forms of political practice immediately encounter (and are then put at risk or repressed by) the deeply reproduced organization of political power in the state, but some others do not, and their relative distance allows something other than simple reproduction. In each case it remains true that such relative distance is in practice only a definition of marginality, within an order still basically directed by the predominant relations. Many relatively alternative conditions of practice survive only within the tolerances of the dominant order, and many again, as they develop and as the distances from otherwise organized relations lessen, are effectively incorporated or face the choice between this and declaring an open opposition.

But the question of relative distance is still crucial in the complex processes of actual reproduction. This can be observed, for example, in religious history. A church can be a highly effective institution of social and cultural reproduction, but there is a crucial social and historical range (definable in terms of relative distance) between a monopoly church (backed, in extreme cases, by state power and even compulsory attendance) and, in one phase, a range of alternative churches, in a later phase the practical possibility of refusal or indifference to any or all of them.

Again, in the development of the family, which is a key reproductive institution, there is a persistent closeness, in our own epoch and in our kinds of culture, between human reproduction and certain social (as distinct from natural) forms of parenthood. But even here variable distances have come to operate, in the possible relations (legal and economic) between husband and wife, and between parents and children, so that not only significantly alternative manifestations of the same basic form but, in certain conditions, some alternative forms have been instituted.

Thus the hypothesis of degree of distance between the conditions of a practice and the most immediately organized forms of social relations seems to be a useful working procedure in the differential sociology of the range of practices which compose a culture and a society. We shall have to look again at the difficult question of the relations between this 'range' and the idea of a whole 'order'. But we can first examine two important questions which are specific to cultural reproduction: the question of relative distance within different types of cultural institution, and the question of the practice (and the limits) of 'reproduction' in cultural forms.

Autonomies and determinations

There has been a long argument within cultural sociology between proponents of (some form of) economic determination of cultural production, and proponents of its relative autonomy. This is clearly a very important argument, but it has been confused by being handled in much too general terms. For it is clear that there are certain kinds of cultural production which are directly economically determined, and it is clear also that there are other kinds which, to say the least, are so indirectly determined, and perhaps in this sense not determined at all, that to approach them in such a way is to misunderstand, reduce and even cancel them. To offer a general theory based on one set of such instances is then as unwise as it is unnecessary. It is here that the hypothesis of relative distances can be particularly important.

Thus it is clear that if, on the one hand, we take cultural

production as the production of newspapers and television programmes, and, on the other hand, as the writing of poems and the making of sculpture, we have to observe, quite apart from the differences between the practices, radically different degrees of distance in their practical conditions.' This is very obvious, but certain kinds of theory have managed to avoid it.

Newspapers and television

In the case of newspapers and television programmes there has been an effectively predominant integration of cultural production with the general conditions of privileged ownership of the means of production and the consequent (wage-labour) employment of the actual producers. Thus, except in certain marginal cases, to practise is to enter these conditions of practice, and certain fundamental kinds of determination, whether (as often) (i) directly economic, or (as again often) (ii) political, in the congruence between the forms of privileged ownership and the general forms of the socio-political order, or more generally (iii) cultural, in an administered compatibility between the actual production and the dominant interests of the social order as seen from just these conditions, then undoubtedly operate.

Minority arts

On the other hand, the conditions of practice of poetry or sculpture, though undoubtedly social conditions and with connections, even here, to the dominant economic and political order, are at a sufficient distance from the general social organization, and especially from the areas of its central concerns, to allow quite practical relative auton-omies and even, at this level, seemingly absolute autonomies.

Variable autonomy

These are, we can say, the two ends of a highly differentiated range. When we look at the writing of fiction, or
the production of plays, we find much more complex
relations. But at this most general level, of the sociology of
cultural reproduction, we find effective distinctions which
should always be included at a very early stage in any
analysis. The material for these distinctions was indicated
in 2, 3 and 4 above, and it can be brought to bear, in any
particular case, not only descriptively but now analytically,
through the hypothesis of variable autonomy, and thus
variable reproduction, according to the degrees of distance
between the conditions of a practice and otherwise
organized social relations.

Internal reproductions

Yet it is clear also that while this takes us some part of the
way, in effective analysis, there are still major problems in
the whole question of reproduction *within* cultural forms.
It is indeed here that the very notion of reproduction, and
the related idea of determination, seems at times to break in
our hands. Certainly, we need a wider range of specifying
descriptions than 'reproduction' alone, even after we have
distinguished its alternative senses, as uniform and genetic,
in other fields. We can perhaps best approach these by
looking at the question of forms.

'Forms'

Our vocabulary for the discussion of forms is radically
diminished and confused. It is a mixed bag of terms from
incompatible bodies of theory: classical, neo-classical,
bourgeois and Marxist. This leads to many difficulties in

theories of art, but perhaps to even more difficulties in the sociology of culture. For what we need, here, is a way of distinguishing different levels of form, as a way of defining what kinds of social relations might be expected to be relevant to them. The matter of levels is also crucial in the consideration of cultural reproduction.

Modes

We can begin by distinguishing two major levels, which have immediate relational importance. At the deepest level we can speak of 'modes' and (if with less certainty) of 'genres' or 'kinds'. What is theoretically critical about this level is that some modes persist (of course through other particular changes) in and through quite different social orders. This does not mean that they were not socially and historically created. Some can be actually dated; not all are universal. But the level of relations involved in them can be more accurately referred to an anthropological or societal dimension than to the sociological in its ordinary sense. Thus the dramatic mode was invented under very specific social conditions, but as a mode it has proved capable of virtually indefinite reproduction in many different social orders. The same is true of the lyrical mode (the non-mimetic composition of a single voice), while the narrative mode is both older and virtually universal. Any of these modes may encounter specific blocks or difficulties in particular cultures. The conventions of drama may be refused or absent, with mimetic actions taken as real or as malevolently illusory. Narrative has recurrent problems of authority and veracity, in the difficult transitions from report and history to fiction. But *as modes*, with highly developed and complex internal signals, which are norm-ally capable of instituting the effective relations within which the form can be shared, they are very general, and their reproduction is at least relatively autonomous.

Significant traditions are established within each, from which new practitioners directly or indirectly learn, and which in effect compose their potential audiences.

Genres

This is often also true, though more narrowly and selectively, of the major kinds or genres. Yet the persistence of tragedy or comedy, epic or romance, is significantly more subject to variation between different epochs and different social orders. Thus neither epic nor romance survived as kinds into the bourgeois epoch, at least without radical redefinition, though they had persisted through other radically variable social orders. In the matter of cultural reproduction we can then offer the hypothesis that reproducible modes may be relatively independent of changes within and even between social orders, while reproducible kinds or genres, though still relatively independent, have some definite dependences on changes between social orders in their epochal sense.

Tied reproduction

Definition of this deep level of cultural reproduction is necessary both to emphasize its general and irreducible significance, and to make a clear space in which we can examine other kinds of formal reproduction. The idea of social and cultural reproduction has in practice been tied to the reproduction of a specific type of social order, usually that of the bourgeois epoch. It is then as well for many reasons to be reminded that there are levels of cultural reproduction and also of cultural production which are not so tied. But of course this should not lead us to saying that the search for ties within an epoch, or within different phases of an epoch, is irrelevant or superficial. For what we then encounter is a different level of reproducible forms. There is already relevant evidence of changes in kinds between epochs, though this is not regular. The really significant changes are at the level of types and then, more specifically (though it is also the normal general term) of forms.

Types

Types can be defined as radical distributions, redistributions and innovations of interest, corresponding to the specific and changed social character of an epoch. The case of bourgeois drama, analyzed in its factors in Chapter 6, is a clear example. There is a directly related case in the realist novel, from the same period, and perhaps also (though this is a very complex case) in the transition from both epic and romance to the general type of 'fiction'. There are other examples – for instance, landscape painting – in other arts. We can then say that these effective general forms (often using persistent modes and either modifying or interacting with persistent kinds) are typical of a particular social order, which in its characteristic relations and distributions of interests continually reproduces them, and of course reproduces them as normal, as 'self-evident' definitions of what various arts should be.

This level of the typical is crucial to the sociology of culture, but it is characteristic that it operates over relatively long periods, within which, while there is undoubtedly an effective reproduction of emphases and interests, directly and indirectly explicable from the character of the epochal order, there are also very significant internal changes, which among other things lead to new forms. The empirical evidence is abundant, but it is difficult to interpret unless we have, first, the working distinctions of levels, in modes, kinds and types, and then, in the matter of form, a more precise understanding of the varieties of reproduction.

Reproducible forms

A form, as we have seen, is inherently reproducible. In a landscape painting or a naturalist play certain formal dispositions – a particular stance, an appropriate selection of subject matter, a specific mode of composition – are in effect given. They are available to the artist as a received way of making his work, and available to others as a set of defined expectations and perceptions. This of course does not mean that the works then produced are identical. That particular sense of reproduction, from mechanical or electronic copying, is entirely misleading. On the other hand, within the given opportunities and limits of the form, there are significant differences of level in the nature of the formal reproduction.

Replication
In large areas of such work there is a process which we might better describe as *replication*, or alternatively propagation or multiplying. It is not that such works are identical, but there is an important sense in which the variations are so trivial that the formal similarities quite outweigh them. There are other cases in which the element of formal reproduction as it were outweighs the specific content. Some term like 'replication' is then necessary, since the body of such work, especially in modern market conditions (where it interlocks in its essential predictability and repeatability with the economic organization of large-scale distribution) is very large indeed. Indeed it is from the evidence of such massive replication that some of the most

convinced propositions of cultural reproduction, especially as applied to large-scale and centralized modern cultural institutions, have been drawn. This is then a very important sense to retain, especially when we note its close ties with reproduction in the modern sense of mechanical and electronic copying, which enables millions of copies of such replicated works to be very widely and rapidly distributed.

Formal production and reproduction

But it would be an error to confine reproduction to these levels. We must indeed refuse the common distinction between 'mass-produced art' – a specific but then not an adequate description of cultural replication – and (as it is usually put) 'original, authentic art'. For there is much 'authentic' art – meaning art of a certain importance, serving more than a passing occasion – which is not 'original' in this Romantic sense. Indeed most of the important art of the world can be properly referred to its shaping forms: forms which it often shares with work now thought unimportant and also, significantly, with the products of replication.

It is in this difficult area that simple notions of reproduction can be especially misleading. Many major works are produced within (and in a way because of the existence of) major forms at the peaks of their cultural development. One common sense of 'reproduction' can diminish these achievements, which in any general theory have to be seen as important *production*, made possible by a reproducible form. Moreover, in cases directly opposite to those in which elements of formal reproduction outweigh specific content, there are important works which are, as it were, a *re-production* of the form: a fuller or newly directed realization of its possibilities. No sense of cultural reproduction is adequate if, limited to replication, it ignores or reduces such cases of formal production and re-production.

Innovations

But we have then also to extend the argument to that important area of cultural history in which, within a still generally reproduced social order, and often within a persistence of what it finds typical, there are decisive formal *innovations*. It is especially necessary here to define levels in reproduction. For there is a reasonable sense in which we can speak of the reproduction of the bourgeois social order from the seventeenth century to our own time, and some theorists have been tempted by the persistence of some of its specifying features (most evident in contrast with other epochs and whole orders) to make this level absolute. But it is characteristic of any social order, as of any active cultural form, that it has continually to be produced as well as reproduced. In this complex process, though there are undoubtedly systematic elements which exert pressures and set limits on the forms of such production and re-production (or there would be no sense in the delineation of a general social order, or in the specification of those elements without which it could not survive and would be replaced), there are also deeply significant internal contradictions, internal shifts and thus internal changes.

In cultural production, these can often be seen as new forms. The breaks to naturalist drama, and then to the alternative forms of subjective and social expressionism, are cases of this kind. Within a certain persistence of typical factors, there were radical alterations of both internal formal elements and of socio-formal relations with audiences and institutions. At times these formal innovations were highly conscious, and were associated with some of the independent formations discussed in 3 above.

In such cases the movement to a new form and to new socio-formal relations is relatively integrated. But specific formal innovations can also happen in relatively isolated work, and then the development of new socio-formal relations can be delayed or even fail.

Transitions

The true process of formal innovation is often difficult to analyse, in specific examples. Obviously when there are sharp breaks these are easier to see, but in practice much formal innovation occurs unevenly and over a protracted period. Often there are transitional periods and works in which what may be primarily evident is that the older form is under strain: that there are incompatible or undigested new elements (cf. the new element of 'self-making' – both the self-made career and the sense of spiritual self-development – and its incompatibility with the received 'inheritance plot', as in George Eliot's *Felix Holt*). The new form, when it comes, is often a simplification to these disturbing elements, and its own full potential can take a considerable time to develop. There are always important works which belong to these very early stages of particular forms, and it is easy to miss their formal significance by comparison with preceding or succeeding mature examples. But for the cultural sociologist these 'transitional' works are very important, since at every other level of analysis, quite properly, attention is centred on the typical, the modal, the characteristic. It is then easy to miss one of the key elements in cultural production: innovation as it is happening; innovation in process. Yet this is one of the very few elements of cultural production to which the stock adjective, 'creative', is wholly appropriate.

Production and reproduction

We have then always to be prepared to speak of production and reproduction, rather than of reproduction alone. Even when we have given full weight to all that can be reasonably described as replication, in cultural as in more general social activities, and when we have acknowledged the systematic reproduction of certain deep forms, we have still to insist that social orders and cultural orders must be seen as being actively made: actively and continuously, or they may quite quickly break down. That some of this making is reproduction, in its narrowest as well as in its broadest sense, is not in doubt. But unless there is also production and innovation, most orders are at risk, and in the case of certain orders (most evidently that of the bourgeois epoch, centred on the drives of capitalist accumulation) at total risk. Thus significant innovations may not only be compatible with a received social and cultural order; they may, in the very process of modifying it, be the necessary conditions of its re-production.

Social processes of innovation

In cultural forms, the most difficult analytic questions centre on the problem of the social processes of innovation. In stable production, and at all the levels of replication, there are usually discoverable social relations of a general and indeed institutional kind. In the case of innovations, the relations are inevitably more complex; some types and examples were discussed in Chapters 3 and 6 above. We can now try to indicate a theoretical framework within which such cases might be analysed, by distinguishing four situations within which innovation can be socially related.

(i) The *rise* of new social classes, or fractions of classes, which bring in new kinds of producer and interest, and/or support new work.

(ii) *Redefinition*, by an existing social class or fraction, of its conditions and relations, or of the general order within which these exist and are changing, so that new kinds of work are necessary.

(iii) *Changes* in the means of cultural production, which provide new formal possibilities; these may or may not be *initially* linked with (i) or (ii).

(iv) *Recognition*, by specifically cultural movements, of the situations indicated in (i) and (ii), at a level preceding or not directly joined to their articulate social organization.

The sociology of culture has hitherto mainly concentrated on cases of type (i), which are indeed numerous. The rise of English bourgeois drama, discussed in Chapter 6 above, is one of many relevant examples. And there are no serious theoretical difficulties in the extension to cases of type (iii), though it should never be assumed that types (i) and (iii) can be assimilated. The remarkable innovations of the cinema, for example – which might reasonably be described as the invention of a new mode, the *cinematic*, interacting with older kinds, types and forms but also undoubtedly creating some important new forms – have ties of many kinds with situations of types (i) and (ii), and at later stages are integrated with stable production and replication, but are also throughout, as innovations, in some important respects direct.

The real theoretical difficulties are in types (ii) and (iv), yet these include very many actual cases. A difficulty in type (i) analysis is that it commonly interprets innovation as 'progressive'; indeed it usually selects its examples by this criterion. But then, in the case of innovations like those of subjective expressionism, there is a problem. They are not the work of a rising class, though they can be related (as in the case of Bloomsbury) to a significantly developing fraction. Yet what such a fraction does, often against the existing core of its class, is to redefine conditions and relations, and to develop new forms, often in ways which (as in Bloomsbury) actively prefigure the next general phase of the class as a whole. This is then in one sense 'progressive', though from different positions, within and outside the class, it is also often called 'decadent'.

Indeed, in cases of type (ii) the social relations between artistic innovation and formed social relationships are primarily indirect, though, as notably in Bloomsbury, there can also be consciousness of the need for quite general redefinition. In cases of type (iv) this indirectness is in effect absolute. It is usually very difficult to demonstrate any manifest relations between such work and otherwise registered social developments since the effective working is more wholly absorbed into the form. Any example will be controversial, but while English Renaissance drama is commonly interpreted, with some reason, in terms of type (i), there are forms within it – the different forms of Shakespearean and of 'Jacobean' tragedy – which seem to me clear cases of type (iv).

Social and cultural change

These points are relevant, finally, to the question of the relations between social and cultural change. In most complex societies we can make crucial sociological differentiations by defining, not only an existing (stable) set of social relations and interests, but also some such sets as dynamic. Thus while we need to define some relatively stable relations of domination and subordination, we have also to see many such relations in their dynamic forms. As a way of analysing these dynamic forms we have then to distinguish the *residual*, the *dominant* and the *emergent*

Dominant

In cultural production the conditions of dominance are usually clear, in certain dominant institutions and forms. These may present themselves as unconnected with dominant social forms, but the efficiency of both depends on their deep integration. Those dominated by such forms usually see them as natural and necessary, rather than as specific forms, while those dominating, in the area of cultural production, may be quite unevenly aware of these practical connections, over a range from conscious control (as of the press and broadcasting), through various kinds of displacement, to a presumed (and then dominant) autonomy of professional and aesthetic values.

Residual and emergent

But then it is also the case that in cultural production both the *residual* – work made in earlier and often different societies and times, yet still available and significant – and the *emergent* – work of various new kinds – are often equally available *as practices*. Certainly the dominant can absorb or attempt to absorb both. But there is almost always older work kept available by certain groups as an extension of or alternative to dominant contemporary cultural production. And there is almost always new work which tries to move (and at times succeeds in moving) beyond the dominant forms and their socio-formal relations.

Levels of reproduction

Cultural reproduction, in its simplest sense, occurs essentially at the (changing) level of the dominant, in all the different ways that have been described. The residual, by contrast, though its immediate processes are reproductive, is often a form of cultural alternative to the dominant in its most recent reproductive forms (cf. the retrospective idea of an 'organic' society, exemplified from certain past literature, as a pre-existing alternative – cultural and then educational and in these terms even political – to modern capitalism and also to modern socialism). At the opposite end of the range, the emergent is related to but not identical with the innovatory. Some kinds of innovation (for example subjective expressionism) are movements and adjustments within the dominant, and become its new forms. But there is usually tension and struggle in this area. Some innovations – kinds of art and thought which emerge and persist as disturbing – would tend to destroy the dominant in any of its forms, just as some new social forces would tend to destroy the social order rather than reproduce or modify it.

No analysis is more difficult than that which, faced by new forms, has to try to determine whether these are new forms of the dominant or are genuinely emergent. In historical analysis the issue gets settled: the emergent becomes the emerged, as in bourgeois drama, and then often the dominant. But in contemporary analysis, just because of the complex relations between innovation and reproduction, the problem is at a different level. To seek help in solving it we have to move to a different set of considerations, within the social organization of culture.

8 Organization

At one level, as we saw in Chapters 2 and 3, we can analyse the social organization of culture in terms of its institutions and formations. At another level, as we saw in Chapters 5 and 6, we can analyse another kind of social organization, in the development of specific arts and forms. The areas analyzed in Chapters 4 and 7 – the means of cultural production, and the process of cultural reproduction – are alternative ways of bringing analyses of these two levels of the social organization of culture into active relations.

We can now explore the possibility of a general concept which, though it should not replace the specific kinds of analysis, might be capable of indicating all their complex interrelations. The modern history of the concept of culture is in fact a history of the search for just such a concept. This is why it is still indispensable in the history and development of social thought. But to the large extent that it reflects without always resolving the difficulties and complexities of this search, and that it often contains without clearly distinguishing alternative and indeed antagonistic conceptions of 'man in society', it needs specification and reinforcement. As we saw in Chapter 1, the strength of its relational range of meanings, from 'whole ways of life' to 'states of mind' and 'works of art', is often in practice its weakness, since its insistence on interrelations can be made passive, or altogether evaded, by its simultaneous possibilities of too wide a generality and too narrow a specialization. To prevent this, by stressing the centrality of its type of definition, we can specify and reinforce the concept of culture as a *realized signifying system*.

Culture as signifying system

To make this clear, we can distinguish a signifying system from, on the one hand, other kinds of systematic social organization, and, on the other hand, more specific signal systems and systems of signs. This distinction is not made to separate and disjoin these areas, but to make room for analysis of their interrelations. Thus it is always necessary to be able to distinguish economic systems, political systems and generational (kinship and family) systems, and to be able to discuss these in their own terms. But when we come, as we must, to interrelate these, we find not only that each has its own signifying system – for they are always relations between conscious and communicating human beings – but that these are necessarily elements of a wider and more general signifying system: indeed a social system.

We have still to be able to discuss a social system in the most general and inclusive terms. It would be wrong to reduce it to the signifying system alone, for this would make all human actions and relationships mere functions of signification and, in doing so, radically diminish them. But it would also be wrong to suppose that we can ever usefully discuss a social system without including, as a central part of its practice, its signifying systems, on which, as system, it fundamentally depends. For a signifying system is intrinsic to any economic system, any political system, any generational system and, most generally, to any social system. Yet it is also in practice distinguishable as a system in itself: as a language, most evidently; as a system of thought or of consciousness, or, to use that difficult alternative term, an ideology; and again as a body of specifically signifying works of art and thought. Moreover all these exist not only as institutions and works, and not only as systems, but necessarily as active practices and states of mind.

The most negotiable meanings of 'culture' are in the distinguishable areas, where a signifying system is at its most manifest. This has been the practical working usage of this book, for it has the advantage of concentrating attention on an area of human practice which is very important in itself and which, as has been argued, has received too little sociological attention. It has the advantage, also, of making room to discuss the specific qualities of these manifest signifying systems, and their relations with what can then be seen as other systems, political, economic and generational. But, at whatever cost in difficulty, it must remain a theoretical control on any such emphasis that these manifest signifying systems – which are often specialized and then quite directly practised, with their own local signal systems and systems of signs – are necessarily, at whatever variations of directness and distance, elements of that wider signifying system which is the condition of any social system, and with which, in practice, they necessarily share their material.

Signifying practice

Thus the distinction of culture, in the broadest or in the narrowest senses, as a realized signifying system, is meant not only to make room for study of manifestly signifying institutions, practices and works, but by this emphasis to activate study of the relations between these and other institutions, practices and work. The key to these relations turns twice. It activates these relations by insisting that signifying practice is deeply present in all those other activities, while preserving the distinction that in those others quite different human needs and actions are substantially and irreducibly present: the necessary signification, as it were, more or less completely dissolved into other needs and actions. It then activates the relations in an opposite direction, by insisting that those other needs and actions are deeply present in all manifest signifying activities, while preserving the distinction that in these practices those other needs and actions are, in their turn, more or less completely dissolved. The metaphor of solution is crucial to this way of looking at culture, and the qualification 'more or less' is not a casual phrase but a way of indicating a true range, in which relatively complete and relatively incomplete degrees of solution, either way, can be practically defined.

Cultural and other practices

Thus the social organization of culture, as a realized signifying system, is embedded in a whole range of activities, relations and institutions, of which only some are manifestly 'cultural'. For modern societies, at least, this is a more effective theoretical usage than the sense of culture as a whole way of life. That sense, derived primarily from anthropology, has the great merit of emphasizing a general system – a specific and organized system of acted and activated practices, meanings and values. It is especially powerful against the habits of separated analysis, historically developed within the capitalist social order, which assume, in theory and practice, an 'economic side of life', a 'political side', a 'private side', a 'spiritual side', a 'leisure side' and so on. Even the weaker forms of connection, in the lives of whole human beings and whole communities, can then be missed altogether, or picked up only under the title of 'interaction' or 'effects', which while they can often be locally registered can never be actively explanatory.

On the other hand, if culture is the 'whole way of life' there can be a crucial absence of significant relational terms beyond it. In practice, in most anthropology, the general relational terms are 'culture' and 'nature', and there are some simple societies in which these are reasonably explanatory, just as there is a very broad sense in which, say, the relations between an 'industrial culture' and its (specifically used) physical world can at the most general levels be investigated and explained. But in highly developed and complex societies there are so many levels of social and material transformation that the polarized 'culture'–'nature' relation becomes insufficient. It is indeed in the area of these complex transformations that the signifying system is itself developed and must be analysed.

Transformations

Some examples of these transformations may indicate the kind of analysis which is possible, in terms of relative degrees of solution. A monetary currency is an obvious example. It is crucial to any system of developed trade, and becomes, in this sense, an economic factor. Yet it is also, evidently, a signifying system, not only of relative economic values but of the area of a specific political order, of which it carries the explicit signs. But while a coinage can be studied as a specific sign-system, and moreover, as in many examples, also analysed aesthetically, there is no real doubt that in any genuine currency the needs and actions of trade and payment are dominant, and the signifying factor, though intrinsic, is in this sense dissolved.

In the case of dwellings, the transformations are more complex. A dwelling begins, not just historically but recurrently, in the area of satisfaction of the most basic need for shelter. But then it is characteristic that a type of dwelling is developed within a particular culture, in full relations not only with its specific physical environment but also with its generational (kinship and family) system, which it thus already signifies. Within further transformations, dwellings come to both embody and signify internal social differentiations, by relative size and position. At this stage, which is always the majority situation, the primary need, as dwelling, is still dominant, in terms of relative comfort and convenience, but it is already mediated by explicit indications – a signifying system – of relative social position. In some cases – palaces, certain kinds of 'country' house – this signifying factor becomes an important factor of design; there are cases in which it has even overridden the normally primary function. The relative importance of the signifying factor is also increased in those rather different cases of an indicated relation between a type of house and a particular (not necessarily dominant) life-style. Again, within and beyond this, domestic architecture becomes a conscious art, with specific aesthetic considerations, and house-dwellers participate in deliberate kinds of enhancement, from decoration to gardening. In a case like this – and the case of dress and clothing is of the same type – there is an especially complex solution of socially developed primary needs, which are always at one level dominant, and of a range of signifying practices, some of them quite manifest.

Modern communications

A modern communications system is yet another series of complex transformations. In a telephone system the factor of direct need – but of a need itself developed by changes in the mode of production and in the consequent patterns of social and family settlement – is relatively dominant. But broadcasting, for example, is quite different. It meets some of the same needs, at a more generalized level, but (as the controversies about its organization have shown and continue to show) it is fundamentally involved with questions of a directly economic and political order, and is often both specifically determined by these and a significant factor in their reproduction and modification. Here then is a case of a manifest signifying system which cannot be treated as if other kinds of need and action were wholly dissolved in it. In fact there is an evident internal range. At one end of this range is news and political opinion, in which the processes of signification – relative importance, relative authority, and more general values – are intensely active, but where it is still essential to see these as quite direct manifestations of a political and economic order. At the other end of the range is 'pure entertainment', where there are still in practice some such direct manifestations but more commonly many kinds of mediation and, in a certain range, practices in which other – external – kinds of need and action are effectively dissolved.

The range of the arts

It is in these difficult transitional areas that most questions about the social organization of culture are centred. The range within broadcasting can be compared with the range within the conscious and specified arts. There seem to be relative degrees of solution in the different arts. Literature, for example, shares its specific medium, language, with the most general medium of all kinds of social communication, and takes much of its material from already manifest areas of other kinds of social action and interest. Attempts have been made to override the resulting problems, for example by the distinction of 'literature' from other forms of writing (cf. Chapter 5). But in practice these are always arguments about the relative autonomy of a particular signifying practice or work, in which the offered categories are themselves forms of signification, with discoverable specific connections to the general signifying system. Yet there is some basis for a relative contrast with, for example, music, in which, though offered categories are still operative and often directive, the specific signifying system seems often to be a more complete solution of other areas and other signifying systems of action and need.

Social organization of culture

Thus the social organization of culture is an extensive and complex range of many types of organization, from the most direct to the most indirect. If we then apply this historically, we have the possibility of developing socio-logical methods in the distinguished but connected areas of cultural institutions, cultural formations, means of cultural production, culturally developed arts and cultural and artistic forms, within our general definitions of cultural production and reproduction as realized and related signifying systems.

Actual analysis can then go in many different directions, and with different local emphases. An empirical sociology of culture, still at so early a stage of development, can be radically extended when these basic problems of theory and method are at least provisionally resolved. That empirical development will of course occur in many specific studies. What may be most useful, here, is to indicate the bearings of this kind of theoretical resolution on one very general and obvious sociological question, where new empirical work is especially necessary. For reasons explained in Chapter 1, there has been a significant amount of work, from outside sociology, in what is effectively the sociology of particular arts, while sociology itself has concentrated on the more evident institutions and on 'effects'. Yet there is one cultural area of direct interest to the most general sociology, in which as yet only a few moves have been made. From the nature of these moves, this area has been defined as that of the social status and social formation of 'intellectuals'.

The sociology of 'intellectuals'

But then the first thing to say is that the definition itself has to be analysed as a term within the signifying system of orthodox sociology. Thus it is commonly asked whether 'intellectuals' can be a 'class', or how, as some other kind of group, they relate or fail to relate to major social classes. There have been some locally useful empirical studies, but in these, and even in the few more developed studies, notably those of Gramsci (translated 1971) and Mannheim (1936 and 1956), there are evidently unresolved theoretical problems which directly affect the methods of inquiry.

The most serious of these is indeed the initial definition of 'intellectuals'. On close examination this turns out to be, first, a misleading specialization from a more general body of cultural producers, and second, a misleading extension from one type of cultural formation to a general social category. For the category 'intellectuals', typically centred on certain kinds of writers, philosophers and social thinkers, in important but uncertain relations with a social order and its major classes, is in fact a very specific historical formation, which cannot be taken as exclusively representative of the social organization of cultural producers. It excludes, on the one hand, those many kinds of artist, performer and cultural producer who cannot reasonably be defined as 'intellectuals' but who quite evidently contribute to the general culture. It excludes, on the other hand, those many kinds of intellectual workers who are directly instituted in the major political, economic, religious and social institutions – civil servants, financial experts, priests, lawyers, doctors – and who are clearly involved, by this fact, not only in their direct practices but also in the production and reproduction of the general social and cultural order. It leaves the definition of teachers, at different levels of education, quite ambiguous, between alternative versions of production and reproduction. It is significant that Gramsci, by contrast for example with Mannheim, moved into the area of these exclusions, with significant effect, but still with the general difficulty of the initial definition of 'intellectuals'.

Intellectuals and intelligence

Interestingly, a recurrent unease in the English usage of 'intellectuals' indicates, on analysis, two of the underlying problems. It is objected, first, that the term is arrogant, because it implies that only intellectuals are intelligent. It is objected, second, that it is a way of defining distance or withdrawal from everyday affairs, and is a kind of rationalization of impracticality. That the occasions and tones of these objections are often silly is not the main point, for they raise, if they cannot resolve, the essential difficulties.

On the first objection it is possible to say, with Gramsci: 'all men are intellectuals . . . but not all men have in society the function of intellectuals.' This has the merit of emphasizing that all human social and productive activities involve intelligence, and that it is then a matter of defining kinds of activity which involve an exceptional degree and regularity of its exercise. But of course this, as Gramsci recognized, takes us well beyond the normal usage of 'intellectuals'. It necessarily includes those intellectual workers who are established in institutions which have direct and indirect purposes other than intellectual work: administrative, financial, legal, political, medical and so on.

Gramsci accepted this, and tried to resolve it with his distinction between 'traditional' and 'organic' intellectuals, where the latter are directly attached to and serving a social class (especially a rising class), while the former are in older and more diverse and often indirect class relations. This points towards the relevant questions, but does not answer them. For we have really to interpret the specific activities and relations, which led to the modern definition of 'intellectuals', by general historical and social principles, rather than let the general principles be defined by extrapolation of more local situations.

Intellectuals and the specialization of ideas

In all societies there are cultural producers, and both their degree of specialization and their consequent social relations are historically determined. We saw different examples of these in Chapters 2 and 3. But then also, whatever the degree of functional specialization at a particular time and place, no aspect of cultural production is itself wholly specialized, for it is always (in different degrees and at different distances, as we saw in Chapter 7) an element of a quite general social and cultural production and reproduction. This is also why the strictly 'intellectual' functions can not be isolated. It is not only that intelligence, in the most general sense, is involved in all social and productive activities. It is also that 'ideas' and 'concepts' – the specialized concerns of 'intellectuals' in the modern sense – are both produced and reproduced in the whole social and cultural fabric at times directly as ideas and concepts, but also more widely in the form of shaping institutions, signified social relations, religious and cultural occasions, modes of work and performance: indeed in the whole signifying system and in the system which it signifies. Moreover, though these general activities of production and reproduction can at one level be analysed as expressing ideas, it is often the case – the historical materialist case – that authentic ideas and concepts are in effect an articulation of what is already being extensively practised, or are effective if uneven interactions with practice. Indeed the 'social system' and the 'signifying system' can only ever be abstractly separated, since they are in practice, over a variable range, mutually constitutive.

Relations of cultural producers

Thus the distinguishable functions of cultural producers can never be understood in isolation from this general production and reproduction, in which all members of a society participate. At the same time this participation is socially and historically variable, to an extreme extent. Its minimum condition is possession and reproduction of a language and customs, and it is almost always in this sense effectively general. But then there are all the degrees of practical domination and subordination, between conquerors and conquered, between social classes, between the sexes, between adults and children. It is inevitable, within such relations of domination and subordination, that the activities of cultural producers become doubly specialized: to a particular kind of cultural work but also to specific attachments within the organized social system.

Cultural producers and dominant groups. It is in general true that these attachments will be to the dominant elements, but this is variable, both in form and degree, according to the nature of the particular kind of dominance. The attachment can be exclusive, so that cultural work is performed only for the dominant group. It can be strategically inclusive, so that while it is performed for everyone it is in the interest of the dominant group. It can also be in mixed forms of these, often as the forms of specialization. But it has also to be emphasized that in certain circumstances of domination and subordination, and in struggles within these, some kinds of cultural work are deliberately produced in and more or less consciously attached to a subordinated group. There is ample evidence of this in the cultures of conquered peoples, of subordinated classes, of subordinated women, and of children. But of course these remain subordinated cultures, if not always (in conditions of struggle not at all) the cultures of subordination. For dominant groups do not always (indeed historically do not often) command the whole signifying system of a people; typically they are dominant *within* rather than over and above it.'

In developing and complex societies there are then markedly uneven relations between cultural producers, now distinguishable as a group or groups, and the general social system. We saw many examples of these variations in Chapters 2 and 3, and we arrived, in Chapter 7, at the hypothesis of relative autonomy – of the practice and then of the practitioners – as a function of the degree of distance from otherwise organized social relations. We can now combine this hypothesis with the further hypothesis (p. 209, above) that institutions and practices can be distinguished by the degree of relative solution of a signifying practice in particular organizations and emphases of action and need. Thus the degree of recognition of relatively autonomous cultural producers, and hence of 'artists' and 'intellectuals' in their modern senses, is a function of the distinction of cultural production 'as such', at certain relative distances from the still quite general and fundamental processes of social and cultural production and reproduction. It is then always a matter of relative distance, to be defined by specific historical and social analysis, rather than a matter of abstract categories or 'spheres'.

Relative distances. The concept of relative distance does

not of course imply *separation*; that is simply one of its extreme examples. There is relative distance in the position of the instituted artists, described in Chapter 2, precisely in their recognition as artists with a prescribed place in the social order. In fact comparable forms of relative distance, by recognition and institution, are historically common. The orders of ecclesiastical clerks, and then the universities, are major examples. Elements of self-organization and of struggle for recognition – often recurrent struggles, in altering general circumstances – are as evident in these as in the guilds and professional organizations of artists.

But relative autonomy by (granted or achieved) recognition and institution, with its often explicit definitions of duties and privileges, is, if not wholly dependent on monopolist types of social order, at least more congruent with them. Even here we can distinguish different kinds of relative autonomy, by types of cultural production. Thus some forms of music and painting, or certain kinds of scholarship and writing, can be given relative autonomy, within a monopolist social order, because they are already internally directed to the reproduction of this order, in its most general terms, or internally directed at least not to contradict or challenge it. And we have only to look at other kinds of work – in law, morality, political theory and relevant kinds of history and scholarship – to see one kind of relative autonomy as a form of functional organization within the social order itself: in effect a division of labour within its production and reproduction.

Churches. The position of the church in feudal societies offers many examples. In a whole series of cases we find what is in effect an integrated relative autonomy, still determined by degrees of relative distance. At some critical points we find a practical overlap between what could now be distinguished as the functions of 'Church' and 'State' intellectuals: intellectuals who are also rulers and administrators. The important cases of tension and of actual conflict, within this integration, then often take the form of tension and conflict *within* the apparently autonomous orders, while tensions and conflicts *between* them are especially associated – as most notably in the English Reformation – with phases of major change in the character of the social order as a whole.

Parties. The position of the political party within modern post-revolutionary societies provides another field for this kind of analysis. It seems to be primarily a form of functional organization within the social order itself, and as such includes intellectuals whose overlap (and intermobility) with state functionaries expresses this fundamental integration. Yet, at relative degrees of distance by types of work, there are still some relative autonomies, in practice governed by internal direction to the reproduction of the general order. In this situation there have been significant cases of tension and conflict *within* the relatively autonomous institutions, but few if any cases of tension and conflict *between* them, while the terms of the current integration hold. For conflict between, say, a communist party and an existing form of communist state organization, which is theoretically predictable, would be definite evidence of major change in the character of the social order as a whole.

Types of integration. Thus relative autonomy is not an abstract condition of any form of cultural institution or practice, but a social and historical variable which is itself largely determined by the type of integration characteristic of the social order as a whole. In conditions in which explicit or practical monopoly has been replaced by phases of dispersed powers, or by explicit conflicts of major social interests, the relations are necessarily more complex.

In situations of dispersed powers the most common relations of cultural producers are those of the different forms of patronage: relative autonomies which are also forms of relative dependence; unestablished plurality as distinct from instituted and internally privileged monopoly. But these developments cannot be separated from changes in the means of production, directly connected with changes in the general social order, which, as in the outstanding case of the market development of publishing and the press, radically altered the terms of immediate relations. At another level, within the same eventual predominance of market conditions, the situation of hitherto relatively privileged institutions, within more directly integrated social orders, altered in complex ways: the universities and the churches are major examples. At each of these levels, and in their interaction, the modern definitions of relative autonomy began to be shaped.

'The uncommitted intelligentsia'

The most influential sociological formulation of these conditions is that of Alfred Weber and of Mannheim: 'a relatively uncommitted intelligentsia' (Mannheim, 1956, 106). This was not intended as an ideal proposition, as in Matthew Arnold and his successors, but as an objective description. In its most careful statements (as distinct from the more widely circulated versions of intellectuals and artists as intrinsically uncommitted, while they are 'real' intellectuals and artists) this is a plausible first response to the evidently altered conditions and their results.

There is indeed no lack of examples of radically independent thinkers and artists, in significantly greater numbers within the liberal state and the predominance of market conditions than within earlier and indeed later kinds of integrated social monopoly These radical independents become the heroes of the definition, and most of us can join in honouring (if not, for the time being, exactly imitating) them. Yet as a *sociological* definition of cultural producers, and of the body of cultural production, it is in effect useless. Indeed it begs the central and very difficult questions of relative autonomy and relative distance, which are the real concerns of cultural sociology, by separating out one type of relationship as normal (and ideal), and then covering this by reducing cultural production and the many kinds of cultural producer to the narrow and self-confirming definition of 'intellectuals'.

Ideologists. On the other hand it cannot be *sociologically* amended by the usual kinds of counter-definition. The most popular of these is the argument that a prevailing social order produces and is reproduced by a general ideology, that the prime carriers and producers of this ideology are the intellectuals (cultural producers), and that cultural work is then (whatever its local forms of organization) definable as the practice of an ideological state apparatus (cf. Althusser, 1971). Qualifications can be made to this argument. The relative autonomy of particular practices can be admitted, by a reasonable emphasis on their forms of internal reproduction. Certain kinds of intellectual work can be designated as 'science', as distinct from the otherwise prevailing 'ideology', though this distinction is normally internal, with no verifiable social conditions for its production. More generally, the empirically unsustainable emphasis on the *state* ideological apparatus can be replaced by the more plausible proposition of control of the ideological apparatus by a dominant *class*, working in general institutional and market terms as well as (or rather than) directly through state organizations. Yet, even with these qualifications, the position falls short of a working sociological theory of cultural production and organization.

Institutional factors. Three kinds of amendment have in fact to be made, and it is significant that these provide initial sociological explanations for the correctly observed phenomena of the Weber-Mannheim definition.

First, there are the specific conditions of asymmetry (discussed in Chapter 4) between a capitalist market and a bourgeois social order. These should not be taken as overriding more general conditions of symmetry or congruity, in the bulk of cultural production, but they exist both generally and at significant transitional points between phases and sectors of the dominant order, making room for a proportion of incongruous, including some valued independent, work.

Second, there are the conditions of internal institutional reproduction, which, as in the notable case of universities, are not necessarily in strict phase with movements of the general order, and which in any case, from the conditions of their original or earlier recognition and privilege, have developed criteria of independent intellectual work which in general seem, and in some cases actually are, bases for original or critical production.

Then, third, a dominent social order of this type does not exclude (though it may – or may regularly seek to – control and modify) important organizations based on different, alternative or oppositional, social and social-class interests. Thus there is always potentially, and in many cases actually, an alternative if limited base for alternative production. All three of these institutional conditions can be empirically investigated, in relation to actual production, of course with historically and locally variable results. Between them they cover much of the divergent cultural production which is (too quickly) described as 'independent' or 'uncommitted'.

Yet of course, most notably in the third case, but also in each of the other two, sociological questions remain to be asked when the reference points have been shifted from the social order as a whole to the more specific operations of the market, the privileged institutions and the alternative or oppositional institutions.

Market asymmetry. Thus the condition of general asymmetry between the market and the established social order has to be related to a number of specific variables. There are observable temporal and sectoral variations, in the actual operations of the market, which constitute one side of this asymmetry. An important contemporary example is specific cultural production for a new young generation (especially marked since the 1950s), where a powerful market force is not matched by any equivalent social or cultural importance or authority in the dominant order. Again there can be viable market sectors, attached to a range of minority or alternative or oppositional groupings, which can function economically in these terms but which are not comparably represented in the explicit institutions of social and cultural authority. Each of these variations produces its own distinguishable formations.

From another direction, especially in the later stages of a market economy, the presumed traditional relations between a market and a social order – where the market could be seen as an economic mechanism within an otherwise persistent national culture – have been put in radical question by the exceptional dynamism of the *cultural* market, provoking crises of authority between traditional institutions – state, educational and religious – and market institutions. Complex sectoral formations then occur within what can still be seen generally as a dominant order and even a dominant class.

Privileged institutions. This interlocks with the sociological detail of the privileged cultural institutions, such as universities. These not only protect certain unsubordinated standards and procedures of cultural work, but under stress protect them differentially. They often have full effect in residual areas (e.g. classical scholarship) by the recognition of relative distance. They usually have functional effect in dominant areas (e.g. applied science) where internal standards and procedures can be accepted as the conditions of effective service. But quite often they have minimal or even negative effect in emergent areas (e.g. critical sociology) where the conditions of privilege may be threatened by their practice, and where the received 'standards' can even be invoked *against* new interests and procedures. This often leads to complex sectoral formations within these institutions, as in our own time in the universities.

But there is a further differentiation. The privilege of certain institutions, beyond the market or beyond the explicit political order, but can be related to the production of independent work, can be related also to a distinction made by Bourdieu (1977), between short-term cultural commerce, as in ordinary market operations, in items of limited symbolic value, and longer-term operations in which major symbolic value is dependent on the slow building of *authority*. At the level of major philosophical, literary and cultural systems, and indeed at a deeper level, of the definition, by selection, of the nature and purposes of cultural work, the privileged institutions – now not only universities but academies, national cultural institutions, public cultural systems – can be seen as indispensable instruments of production of the ideas and practices of an authoritative order, and have often to be seen as such even when, as an internal condition of their long-term authority, they include minority elements of dissent or opposition.

Alternative and oppositional formations. The case of cultural work in or for alternative or oppositional organizations is different, but has its own sociological variables. In the case of an established class or interest, we can observe settled degrees of distance, as of inner and outer circles, between cultural and intellectual work and the interests it serves. This can be discerned organizationally and also analysed in the sense of Bourdieu's distinction between short-term and long-term operations. Many of the same considerations apply to alternative or oppositional organizations which have become relatively established, but the determining sociological difference is that the mode of relative establishment – and then of alternative and oppositional kinds of cultural work – is itself a function of the relations between an alternative or oppositional interest and the existing generally dominant interest. For to the degree that alternative or oppositional work can be incorporated, if still as distinctive elements, in the social and cultural system as a whole, the relatively settled degrees of distance can persist.

On the other hand, any movement towards transformation or replacement of the existing system provokes forms of internal as well as the more evident and often drastic forms of external crisis. Sectoral complexities often occur *within* a radical intelligentsia, notably because the directors of a genuinely oppositional party are themselves not a ruling class but in a complex intermediate position between a potential governing system and active cultural production. The otherwise settled degrees of distance, as between 'intellectual leaders of the party', 'party intellectuals', 'intellectuals associated with the party', 'intellectuals serving the interest which the party also serves', 'intellectuals giving authority to the long-term interest and perspective of the class and of the class as transforming society', are much more difficult to negotiate in genuinely oppositional than in established or relatively established parties: both because of the presence and urgency of actual conflict, and because of unresolved inter-sectoral definitions. These are the complex realities explored in Gramsci's (translated 1971) analyses of 'hegemony' and of 'organic' intellectuals. In practice they now constitute the most difficult problems of alternative and oppositional cultural work.

Historical changes

We have then greatly expanded the sociological terms of reference within which the problem of 'the intellectuals', and more generally of all kinds of cultural producer, can be specifically analysed. In particular we have shifted the relevant concepts, arguments, and modes of research and inquiry, beyond the conditioned received terms. We can now conclude with some more general historical and contemporary considerations.

Cultural minorities

First, the received categories of broad cultural description – 'aristocratic' and 'folk', 'minority' and 'popular', 'educated' and 'uneducated' – have to be related, as social products, to social transformations which have outdistanced them, or of which they were always a misrepresentation. The early categories had distinct social bases, in feudal and immediately post-feudal societies, and this was still relatively true of the early and middle stages of modern class societies. The significant transition occurred when intellectual and artistic activities were grouped and abstracted in their own terms, without significant correlation with other kinds of social organization. This is a characteristic phenomenon of bourgeois society, in which there are of course 'minority' arts and intellectual pursuits, and in which there are – as still in the press – some effective 'minority' sectors. But the relation between these and any more general socio-cultural organization has been problematic since the period of industrial urbanization, and acutely problematic since the period of universal education and general suffrage.

It was within these specific problems that the concepts of the 'educated' or 'cultivated' minority – without manifest or reliable correlations with other kinds of social organization – and then of a special category of 'intellectuals' were formed. Yet the real dynamics of the socio-cultural process are most evident in the transformations of 'popular', which moved not only along a trajectory from late forms of 'folk' culture to new and partly self-organizing forms of urban popular culture, but also along a trajectory of extended – and finally massively extended – production of 'popular' culture by the bourgeois market and by state educational and political systems.

Popular culture

At one level, 'popular culture', in these later periods, is a very complex combination of residual, self-made and externally produced elements, with important internal conflicts between these. At another level, and increasingly, this 'popular' culture is the major area of bourgeois and ruling-class cultural production, moving towards an offered 'universality' in the modern communications institutions, with a 'minority' sector increasingly seen as residual and to be formally 'preserved' in those terms. Thus a relatively undisputed 'high culture' has been quite generally moved into the past tense, with some attendant and competing successor minorities of a discrete kind, while the active and effective 'minority', within a class-determined range of cultural production, has moved decisively into the general 'majority' area.

Bureaucracies

Thus especially since universal education and general
suffrage there has been a reconstitution of cultural
organization, with some residual direct class elements but
with dominance defined at an essentially general level.
There has been a major expansion of cultural and
educational bureaucracies, over and above the artists and
teachers whom they typically employ. Moreover these
bureaucracies have interlocked – not without some local
conflicts – with the political, economic and administrative
bureaucracies, in ways that undoubtedly compose an
organizing – a realized signifying – system. The sheer scale
of cultural production, of all kinds, has thus – though
allowing for local minority sectors and containing, within
itself, some degrees of variable distance – transformed the
types of organization and the corresponding concepts on
which earlier descriptions had been based. It can then be
said that while there is innovatory work in many forms of
art and thought, the genuinely emergent has to be defined
not only in specific terms but primarily in terms of
contributions to alternatives to this dominant general
system.

Extended markets

The second major historical development, radically
affecting cultural organization, is the institution, especially
marked in some media, of an international and even a world
market. Except in some, mostly early, forms of closed or
self-subsistent societies, the processes of cultural import
and export have always been important. They can be
interpreted generally as the spread of art and ideas, but
there are often significant sociological variables in the
actual processes. Decisions about what to import, and
when, are often very similar to the processes of a selective
tradition, when elements of the past are deliberately

reintroduced or revived. Sometimes the importing is done by dominant groups, as in the case of the English Restoration, with its deliberate importation of aristocratic French forms. Sometimes, on the other hand, it is done by an alternative or oppositional group, as in the recent case of the importation of a range of continental Marxist works by the English New Left. The sociological specifics of these import patterns have never been adequately investigated, mainly because they are overridden by general formulas, which often of course have some substance, of getting to know the best work of other societies. Yet the selective processes involved must always be evident, and we should at least look to see if there are discoverable connections between the modes of selective import and strictly internal social relations.

Cultural exports
Cultural export is a different process. Typically it is a function of relative political or commercial dominance, with especially clear cases in the political empires and many related cases in general international competition. But changes in the means of production and distribution have transformed many of these older processes. In certain areas, notably cinema and television production, conditions of relative monopoly, not only internally but internationally, have led beyond simple processes of export to more general processes of cultural dominance and then of cultural dependence. These new relations, notably studied by Schiller (1969), are not confined to the immediate works that are exported. They have radical effects on the specific signifying systems that are national languages. They carry wide areas of cultural and ideological emphasis. They can be directly related to wider commercial operations, specifically through advertising, and to general political operations. In their very process

they lead to new forms of 'multinational' cultural combine, including the takeover or implantation of nationally based forms. Thus the sociology of cultural organization, typically developed for single-society systems, has to be radically extended to this new and increasingly important system of combined and uneven cultural production on a trans-national and para-national scale.

Information processes

The third major historical development is within the general complex of labour processes, where fundamental changes have radically affected the definition of cultural production. We can of course still distinguish the productive operations of the traditional cultural forms: music, painting, sculpture, drama, poetry, and so on. But there have been historical periods in which these, together with learning and scholarship, could be relatively clearly distinguished from other, directly productive work, in agriculture and manufactures, and in the distribution of their products. At the most specific level they can still be so distinguished, but meanwhile, and at a rapidly increasing rate, the majority of labour processes have been transformed. In advanced industrial societies direct production, in the older senses, now often involves a quite small and declining proportion of the working population. Distribution involves many others, but in modern marketing conditions, and with the increasing importance of large-scale economic organizations, information processes, both external and internal, have become a qualitative part of economic organization. At the same time, within the modern administrative state, and within modern political systems, information processes have become so central, again in both external and internal systems, that here also the general character of these operations has qualitatively changed. Thus a major part of the whole modern labour process must be defined in terms which are not easily theoretically separable from the traditional 'cultural' activities. Precise estimates are not easy to make, because of the integration and complexity of the processes, but a recent American calculation offered a figure of fifty per cent of the working population involved in specific information processing and handling. Whatever the actual proportion may be, there can be little doubt that the production and distribution of ideas and information has acquired a quite new importance in most kinds of work.

Thus, not only at the level of vastly expanded cultural consumption, itself a qualitative change from earlier more limited or more occasional forms, but also at the level of forms of cultural production and distribution, we have moved into a radically altered situation. Within this, it is true, many of the older types of determination – in state power or in economic property and command – are still decisive, though they have often to amend and even (as in the amendment of politics by modern kinds of electoral process) change their forms to survive. On the other hand, so many more workers are involved in the direct operations and activations of these systems that there are quite new social and social-class complexities. The dependence of established power groups on these working systems has become very great, and it is significant that some of the most bitter 'industrial' conflicts and struggles are now in this critical area of information systems, of communications and of administration based on data collection and processing. Thus the whole system of cultural production and reproduction is at risk in some quite new ways, because of these fundamental changes in the character and distribution of labour processes.

Altered and alterable relations

Moreover, the altered and potentially alterable relations of such a system cannot be confined to an operational level. Many of the techniques and some of the skills of cultural production, in its widest sense, are now necessarily more generally disseminated. The social character of cultural production, which is evident in all periods and forms, is now more directly active and inescapable than in all earlier developed societies. There are then persistent and major contradictions between this central social character of cultural production and, on the one hand, the residual forms of specific cultural production and, on the other hand, the still determining forms of political and economic control.

Thus, while cultural sociology has many kinds of work within its immediate grasp – in the analysis of institutions and formations, and of signifying systems and forms – it must also necessarily be involved with these active contemporary relations, in a social order now more directly based on a practical generalization of its specific processes and concerns. A fully responsible sociology of culture, itself significantly developing at just this point of general change, has then to be analytically constructive as well as constructively analytic. But it can still only be either, if by extending collaborative work it learns how to become, against many difficulties and resistances, a new major discipline.

Bibliography

ADORNO, T. W (1949): *Philosophie der neven Musik*, Frankfurt.

ADORNO, T. W. (1967a): 'Thesen zur Kunstsoziologie', *Kölner Zeitschrift für Soziologie und Sozialpsychologie*, XIX, 1.

ADORNO, T. W (tr. 1967b): *Prisms*, Spearman, London.

ALBRECHT, M. C. (1968): 'Art as an Institution', *American Sociological Review*, XXXIII, 3.

ALBRECHT, M. C., BARNETT, J. H. and GRIFF, M., eds. (1970): *The Sociology of Art and Literature*, Duckworth, London.

ALTHUSSER, L. (tr. 1970): *For Marx*, Penguin, Harmondsworth.

ALTHUSSER, L. (tr. 1971): *Lenin and Philosophy*, New Left Books, London

ALTHUSSER, L. (tr 1976): *Essays in Self-Criticism*, New Left Books, London.

ALTICK, H. D (1957): *The English Common Reader*, Cambridge University Press.

ANDERSON, P. (1968): 'Components of the National Culture', *New Left Review*, 50.

ANTAL, F. (1947): *Florentine Painting and its Social Background*, Kegan Paul, London.

BAKHTIN, M. (1968): *Rabelais and his World*, MIT Press, Cambridge, Massachusetts.

BALIBAR, R. (1974): *Les Français fictifs*, Hachette, Paris.

BANN, S. and BOWLT, S., eds. (1973): *Russian Formalism*, Scottish Academic Press, Edinburgh.

BARNETT, J. H. (1958): 'Research Areas in the Sociology of Art', *Sociology and Social Research*, LXII, 6.

BARNETT, J. H. (1959): 'The Sociology of Art' in R. K. Merton *et al.*, *Sociology Today*, Basic Books, New York.

BARRETT, M. *et al.*, eds. (1979): *Ideology and Cultural Production*, Croom Helm, London.

BARTHES, R. (1957): *Mythologies*. Seuil, Paris

BARTHES, R. (tr. 1977): *Image, Music, Text*, Fontana, London.

BAXANDALL, L. (1972): *Radical Perspectives in the Arts*, Penguin, Harmondsworth.

BAXANDALL, L. and MORAWSKI, S., eds. (1973): *Marx and Engels on Literature and Art*, Telos Press, St Louis, Missouri.

BELJAME, A. (1948): *Men of Letters and the English Public in the Eighteenth Century*, Kegan Paul, London.

BENJAMIN, W. (tr. 1969): *Illuminations*, Harcourt Brace, New York.

BENJAMIN, W. (tr. 1973): *Baudelaire*, New Left Books, London.

BENNETT, T. (1979): *Formalism and Marxism*, Methuen, London.

BERELSON, B. (1950): *Content Analysis in Communications Research*, Free Press, Glencoe, Illinois.

BIGSBY, C. W. E., ed. (1976): *Approaches to Popular Culture*, Arnold, London.

BLOCH, M. *et al.* (1977): *Aesthetics and Politics*, New Left Books, London.

BLUMLER, J. and McQUAIL, D., eds. (1968): *Television in Politics*, Faber, London.

BOURDIEU, P. and PASSERON, J-C. (1977): *Reproduction in Education, Society and Culture*, Sage, London.

BRYSON, L., ed. (1948): *The Communication of Ideas*, New York.

BURCKHARDT, J. C. (tr. 1878): *The Civilization of the Period of the Renaissance in Italy*, London.

BURKE, P. (1974): *Tradition and Innovation in Renaissance Italy*, Fontana, London.

CAUDWELL, C. (1938): *Illusion and Reality*, Lawrence and Wishart, London.

CAUDWELL, C. (1965): *The Concept of Freedom*, Lawrence and Wishart, London.

CLARK, T. J. (1973): *Image of the People*, Thames and Hudson, London.

COLLINS, A. S. (1928): *The Profession of Letters*, Routledge, London.

CORRADI, I. (1971): 'Cultural Dependence and the Sociology of Knowledge', *International Journal of Comparative Sociology*, VIII, 1.

COWARD, R. (1977): 'Class, Culture and the Social Formation', *Screen*, XVIII, 1.

CREEDY, J., ed. (1970): *The Social Context of Art*, Tavistock, London

CURRAN, J., GUREVITCH, M. and WOOLLACOTT, J., eds. (1977): *Mass Communication and Society*, Arnold, London.

DILTHEY, W. (tr. 1976): *Selected Writings*, ed. Rickman, H. P., Cambridge University Press.

DUNCAN, H. D. (1947) . *Annotated Bibliography on the Sociology of Literature*, Chicago University Press.

DUVIGNAUD, J. (1965): *Sociologie du théâtre*, PUF, Paris.

DUVIGNAUD, J. (1967): *Sociologie de l'art*, PUF, Paris.

EAGLETON, T. (1976): *Criticism and Ideology*, New Left Books, London.

ENZENSBERGER, H. M. (tr. 1970): 'Constituents of a Theory of the Media', *New Left Review*, 64.

ERLICH, V. (tr. 1955): *Russian Formalism*, Mouton, The Hague.

ESCARPIT, R. (tr. 1966): *The Book Revolution*, Harrap, London.

ESCARPIT, R. (tr. 1971): *The Sociology of Literature*, Cass, London.

ESSEX UNIVERSITY (1971): *Literature, Society and the Sociology of Literature*, University of Essex, Colchester.

FISCHER, E. (tr. 1963): *The Necessity of Art*, Penguin, Harmondsworth.

FISCHER, E. (tr. 1969): *Art against Ideology*, Penguin, Harmondsworth.

FRANCASTEL, P. (1965): *Peinture et société*, Gallimard, Paris.

FRANCASTEL, P. (1970): *Études de sociologie de l'art*, Denoel, Paris.

FRAZER, J. G. (1890): *The Golden Bough*, Macmillan, London.

FRYE, N. (1957): *Anatomy of Criticism*, Princeton, New Jersey.

GARNHAM, N. (1977): 'Towards a Political Economy of Culture', *New Universities Quarterly*, Summer.

GERBNER, G. ed. (1977): *Mass Media in Changing Cultures*, Wiley, New York.

GLASGOW UNIVERSITY MEDIA GROUP (1976): *Bad News*, Routledge, London.

GLASGOW UNIVERSITY MEDIA GROUP (1980): *More Bad News*, Routledge, London.

GOLDMANN, L. (1964): *The Hidden God*, Routledge, London.

GOLDMANN, L. (1970): *Marxisme et sciences humaines*, Gallimard, Paris.

GOLDMANN, L. (1975): *Towards a Sociology of the Novel*, Tavistock, London.

GOLDMANN, L (1976): *Cultural Creation*, Telos Press, St Louis, Missouri.

GOMBRICH, E. (1963): *Meditations on a Hobby Horse*, Phaidon, London

GRAMSCI, A. (tr. 1971) *Selections from the Prison Notebooks*, Lawrence and Wishart, London.

HALL, S. and WHANNEL, P. (1964): *The Popular Arts*, Hutchinson, London.

HALL, S. (1977): 'Culture, the Media and the Ideological Effect' in Curran, J. *et al.*, *Mass Communication and Society*, Arnold, London.

HALLORAN, J. (1970): *The Effects of Television*, Panther, London.

HALLORAN, J., BROWN, R. L. and CHANEY, D. (1970): *Television and Delinquency*, Leicester University Press.

HAUSER, A. (1962): *The Social History of Art*, Routledge, London.

HEATH, S. and SKIRROW, G. (1977): 'Television, a World in Action', *Screen*, XVIII, 2.

HENNING, E. B. (1960): 'Patronage and Style in the Arts', *Journal of Aesthetics and Art Criticism*, XVIII.

HERDER, J. G. (tr. 1968): *Reflections on the Philosophy of the History of Mankind*, Chicago University Press.

HIMMELWEIT, H., OPPENHEIM, A. and VINCE, P. (1958): *Television and the Child*, Oxford University Press.

HOGGART, R. (1957): *The Uses of Literacy*, Chatto and Windus, London.

HORKHEIMER, M. and ADORNO, T., intro. (1973): *Aspects of Sociology*, Heinemann, London.

HORKHEIMER, M. (1968): *Kritische Theorie*, Frankfurt.

HUET, A., *et al.* (1978): *Capitalisme et industries culturelles*, Grenoble.

HUGHES, H. S. (1959): *Consciousness and Society*, MacGibbon and Kee, London.

INGLIS, F. (1972): *The Imagery of Power*, Heinemann, London.

JAMESON, F. (1972a): *Marxism and Form*, Princeton University Press, New Jersey.

JAMESON, F. (1972b): *The Prison House of Language*, Princeton University Press, New Jersey.

JAY, M. (1973): *The Dialectical Imagination*, Heinemann, London.

JUNG, C. G. (1933): *Modern Man in Search of a Soul*, Kegan Paul, London.

KAUTSKY, K. (1927): *The Materialist Conception of History*, London.

KAVOLIS, V. (1968): *Artistic Expression : a sociological analysis*, Cornell University Press, Ithaca, New York.

KELLY, G. (1976): *The English Jacobin Novel*, Oxford University Press.

KLINGENDER, F (1972): *Art and the Industrial Revolution*, Paladin, St Albans.

KRACAUER, S. (1947): *From Caligari to Hitler*, Princeton University Press, New Jersey.

KROEBER, A. L. and KLUCKHOHN, C. (1952): 'Culture: a Critical Review of Concepts and Definitions', *Peabody Museum Papers*, XLVII, Harvard University Press.

LASSWELL, H. D. (1948): 'The Structure and Function of Communication in Society' in Bryson, L., *The Communication of Ideas*, New York.

LAURENSON, D. T. and SWINGEWOOD, A. (1972): *The Sociology of Literature*, MacGibbon and Kee, London.

LAZARSFELD, P. and MERTON, R. (1948): 'Mass Communication, Popular Taste and Organized Social Action' in Bryson, L., ed., *op. cit.*

LAZARSFELD, P. and STANTON, S., eds. (1949): *Communication Research*, New York.

LAZARSFELD, P. and KATZ, E. (1955): *Personal Influence*, Free Press, Glencoe, Illinois.

LEAVIS, F. R. (1962): *The Common Pursuit*, Penguin, Harmondsworth.

LOWENTHAL, L. (1957): *Literature and the Image of Man*, Boston.

LOWENTHAL, L. (1961): *Literature, Popular Culture and Society*, Prentice-Hall, Englewood Cliffs, New Jersey.

LUKÁCS, G. (tr. 1950): *Studies in European Realism*, Hillway, London.

LUKÁCS, G. (tr. 1962): *The Historical Novel*, Merlin, London.

LUKÁCS, G. (1969): *Die Eigenart des Ästhetischen*, Frankfurt.

LUKÁCS, G. (tr. 1971): *Theory of the Novel*, Merlin, London.

MACHEREY, P. (1978): *A Theory of Literary Production*, Routledge, London.

MANNHEIM, K. (1936): *Ideology and Utopia*, Routledge, London.

MANNHEIM, K. (1956): *Essays on the Sociology of Culture*, Routledge, London.

MAO, TSE-TUNG (tr. 1960): *On Art and Literature*, Foreign Languages Press, Peking.

MARCUSE, H. (1978): *The Aesthetic Dimension*, Macmillan, London

MARTINDALE, D. (1962): *Social Life and Cultural Change*, Van Nostrand, Princeton, New Jersey.

MARX, K. and ENGELS, F. (tr. 1970): *The German Ideology*, Lawrence and Wishart, London.

MARX, K. (tr. 1973): *Grundrisse*, Penguin, Harmondsworth.

MATTELART, A. (1976): *Multinationales et systèmes de communication*, Paris.

MAYER, J. P (1948): *British Cinemas and their Audiences*, Dobson, London.

McQUAIL, D. (1975): *Communication*, Longman, London.

MORAWSKI, S. (1974): *Fundamentals of Aesthetics*, MIT Press, Cambridge, Massachusetts.

MUKAROVSKY, J. (1970): *Aesthetic Function, Norm and Value as Social Fact*, Ann Arbor.

MULHERN, F. (1979): *The Moment of Scrutiny*, New Left Books, London.

MURDOCK, G. and GOLDING, P. (1974): *For a Political Economy of Communication*, Merlin, London.

NIETZSCHE, F. (1872): *Die Geburt der Tragödie ans dem Geiste der Musik*, Leipzig.

PLEKHANOV, G. (tr 1953): *Art and Social Life*, Lawrence and Wishart, London.

READ, H. (1936): *Art and Society*, Faber, London.
ROCKWELL, J. (1974): *Fact in Fiction*, Routledge, London.
RUSKIN, J. (1851–6): *The Stones of Venice*, London.
RUSKIN, J. (1857): *The Political Economy of Art*, London.
ROSSI-LANDI, F. (1978): *L'Ideologia*, Isedi, Milan.

SCHILLER, H. (1969): *Mass Communications and American Empire*, Kelly, New York.
SCHILLER, H. (1976): *Communication and Cultural Domination*, International Arts and Sciences Press, New York.
SEWTER, A. C. (1935): 'The Possibilities of a Sociology of Art', *Sociological Review*, XXVII.
SIEBERT, F., PETERSON, T. and SCHRAMM, W. (1956): *Four Theories of the Press*, Urbana, Illinois.
SILBERMANN, A. (1968): 'Introductory Definitions of the Sociology of Art', *International Social Science Journal*, XX, 4.
SMITH, M. W. ed. (1961): *The Artist in Tribal Society*, Routledge, London.
SOROKIN, P. A. (1937): *Social and Cultural Dynamics*, American Book, New York.

THOMPSON, E. P. (1955): *William Morris*, Lawrence and Wishart, London.
THOMPSON, E. P. (1963): *The Making of the English Working Class*, Gollancz, London.
THOMPSON, E. P. (1979): *The Poverty of Theory*, Merlin, London.
THOMSON, G. (1941): *Aeschylus and Athens*, Lawrence and Wishart, London.
TODOROV, T., ed. (1965): *Théorie de la littérature*, Seuil, Paris.
TOMARS, A. S. (1940): *Introduction to the Sociology of Art*, Mexico City.
TUNSTALL, J. (1977): *The Media are American*, Constable, London.

VAZQUEZ, A. S. (1973): *Art and Society*, Monthly Review Press, New York.

VICO, G. (tr. 1948). *New Science*, Cornell University Press.

VOLOSINOV, V. (1973): *Marxism and the Philosophy of Language*, Seminar, New York.

WEBER, A. (1951): *Principien der Geschichts und Kultursoziologie*, Munich

WEBER, A. (tr. 1958): *The Rational and Social Foundations of Music*, Urbana, Illinois.

WEINBERG, M. (1962): *TV in America*, Ballantine, New York.

WESTON, J. L. (1920): *From Ritual to Romance*, Cambridge University Press.

WHITE, L. (1947): *The American Radio*, Chicago University Press.

WILLIAMS, R. (1958): *Culture and Society*, Chatto and Windus, London.

WILLIAMS, R. (1961): *The Long Revolution*, Chatto and Windus, London.

WILLIAMS, R. (1962): *Communications*, Penguin, Harmondsworth.

WILLIAMS, R. (1974): *Television: Technology and Cultural Form*, Fontana, London.

WILLIAMS, R. (1976): *Keywords*, Fontana, London.

WILLIAMS, R. (1977): *Marxism and Literature*, Oxford University Press.

WILLIAMS, R. (1980): *Problems in Materialism and Culture*, New Left Books, London.

WRIGHT, C. R. (1959): *Mass Communication*, Random House, New York.

WOLLEN, P. (1972): *Signs and Meanings in the Cinema*, Secker and Warburg, London.

Index

Index

Fontana Modern Masters
Editor: Frank Kermode

Barthes
Second Edition

Jonathan Culler

Roland Barthes (1915–80) was an 'incomparable enlivener of the literary mind' whose lifelong fascination was with 'the way people make their world intelligible'. He has a multi-faceted claim to fame: to some he is the structuralist who outlined a 'science of literature', and the most prominent promoter of semiology; to others he stands not for science but for pleasure, espousing that literature which gives the reader a creative role. He championed the *Nouveau Roman* but his best known works deal with classic writers such as Racine and Balzac. He called for 'the death of the author', urging that we study not writers but texts; yet he himself published idiosyncratic books rightly celebrated as imaginative products of a personal vision.

Professor Culler elucidates the varied theoretical contributions of this 'public experimenter' and describes the many projects which Barthes explored and which helped change the way we think about a range of cultural phenomena, from literature, fashion, wrestling and advertising to notions of the self, of history and of nature.

In this new, updated version of his original study, Professor Culler has expanded the bibliography to include the latest works published by and about Roland Barthes, both in French and in English.

Fontana Press

Fontana Modern Masters
Editor: Frank Kermode

Chomsky
Third Edition

John Lyons

Chomsky's contribution to the study of language has, over the last four decades, been enormous, and has influenced those working in many disciplines, including the other cognitive sciences. Language is, arguably, an even more distinctively human characteristic than intelligence, and the thousands of different human languages are, according to Chomsky, cut to the same general pattern. This pattern is determined, he claims, by innate structuring principles which only human beings possess. Chomsky's search for the universal in language has revitalized the question of the relationship between language and mind, and has provided a powerful new tool, generative grammar, for students of language.

In this Third Edition of his concise, accessible introduction to Chomsky's work, John Lyons has added an extensive final chapter which seeks to assess the continuing ramifications of the Chomskyan Revolution in linguistics today. He has also thoroughly updated the bibliographies – both of Chomsky's own prolific output and of the multiplying secondary material – and the biographical note, in order fully to arm any prospective explorer of Chomsky's *oeuvre* with all the relevant resources they may need.

'John Lyons' book on Chomsky is simply the best short introduction in the English language. It is within the grasp of an intelligent layman. Anyone who reads it will understand the elements of transformational grammar, and be able to follow current controversies.'

Leonard Jackson, *Times Educational Supplement*

'Lyons' account is itself a minor modern masterpiece of compression and clarity.'

Alan Ryan, *New Society*

Fontana Press